Pablo Neruda School, Reggio Emilia, Italy, 1992. — Photo: SGC
Children sculpting their teacher's head while atelierista, Mara Davoli, documents their work.

SEEING YOUNG CHILDERN WITH NEW EYES:

What we've learned from Reggio Emilia about children and ourselves

Sydney Gurewitz Clemens
& Leslie Gleim
with Jed Handler

Early Reviewers comment:

Dear Sydney,

I want to congratulate you and Leslie on your wonderful new book. You introduce the reader to Reggio Emilia thinking in a most engaging way. Great title!

I am so glad that you persisted with your vision and I wish you every success with the book.

Ursula Kolbe, Australia

Author, *Rapunzel's Supermarket: All about Young Children and their Art*

Using real life experiences of early childhood professionals and the children with whom they work, **Seeing Young Children with New Eyes explains** the philosophy and theories of Dr. Loris Malaguzzi and his colleagues in language that is engaging and understandable to both early childhood professionals and to non-professionals. They delve into the concept of the "Image of the Child" and how, by respecting children and allowing them to explore and create with a multitude of media, we can provide them with richness of "languages" in which to discover new ideas and express themselves.

The authors provide insight into how the concept of the "Image of the Child" can be made compatible within the culture of the United States and the many regulations and standards which early education and care professionals must abide by. They provide practical strategies on how to operationalize the Reggio Emilia philosophy and theories within these constraints.

Seeing Young Children with New Eyes is a must read for all early education and care professionals as well as for all those who care about young children's development.

Deborah Abelman, Ph.D.

Early Childhood Education Supervisor at Family Service of Greater Boston

It is the first book that truly speaks from personal teaching experiences and parental experiences that are laid out and successfully illustrate the potential of children. That is missing in so many books in our field. Sometimes the experiences are found in sidebars or boxes with a special color. They are not personalized but are a summary of what is important to the point at hand and always have that "ECE textbook college course" feeling in them. One witnesses the evolution of the teacher as experiences are woven into the book from the onset which keeps the reader reading.

Claudia Chamberland, B.A., M.A., NAMC, Canada

CONTENTS

INTRODUCING THE BOOK

Preface

> *Our goal is to build an amiable school where children, teachers,*
> *and families feel at home. Such a school requires careful thinking*
> *and planning concerning procedures, motivations, and interests.*
> — Dr. Loris Malaguzzi

Dr. Malaguzzi was the educational thinker who guided and inspired the Reggio Emilia schools from their birth in 1945 until his death in 1994.

> *Imagination*
> *is what enables us to cross the empty spaces*
> *between ourselves and those...*
> *we have called 'other' over the years.*
> — Maxine Greene[1]

This is a book for early childhood teachers who are able to imagine their teaching growing better over time, and who are willing to struggle to make what they imagine come true. It's for teachers who can imagine that offering a good learning experience to children will, in some way, help the world progress towards peace and justice, and insist that all people will be included in their goodwill.

More than two decades ago, when my Pacific Oaks colleague Dr. Elizabeth Jones handed me the Reggio Emilia video *To Make a Portrait of a Lion* and a single page of notes, I was inspired to study more about how young children are educated in Reggio Emilia. I have learned that this is a continuing task I will embrace for the rest of my life; just as teaching practices in Reggio shift, evolve, and grow steadily.

I have come to realize that Reggio thinking depends on so many variables that each of us re-invents it in her[2] own way, drawing from her own cultural vocabulary and conventions, constantly revising and expanding.

Now no longer teaching children, I wanted to write a book about my discoveries along the Reggio Emilia road, and having written other books about teaching, realized combining my thoughts with those of another teacher actively practicing in the classroom would bring the reader two perspectives and two processes, providing wider, deeper, and hopefully, richer views.

Thus Leslie Gleim's involvement and the tales from her Ohio classroom and experience broaden the scope of what I provide, as her children dance through these pages. We mean for each reader to discover her own personal individual path, and not feel bound to copy either of ours. Please, make this material your own!

---

1. From Greene, M. 1995 *Release the Imagination: Essays on education, the arts, and social change. San Francisco: Jossey-Bass. Page 3.*
2. There are so many more women in our field, and "his/her" is truly awkward on the written page, thus my choice of alternating pronouns..

Reading this book

We began reading and going to workshops, and started to think in Reggio Emilia terms (a few pages further on we'll tell you more about the city of Reggio Emilia). We were excited by them, and that led us to try to understand the rich, full, Image of the Child they've developed. In Part One we explore many aspects of the Image of the Child.

We began collecting data – photos, artworks, transcripts of children's language – learning a Documentation Process that assists us with planning and helps us realize and grow toward our potential while helping children see the vastness of the worlds of possibility and the purpose of research. We write about this Documentation Process in Part Two.

We refined our ability to look at what's happening from the child's perspective, aligning our viewpoints with theirs. We write about this in Part Three.

We learned to be reflective, to throw away old practices that didn't serve our communities. We learned to work together with other adults in more productive ways. This is in Part Four.

We learned new ways of giving children assistance in their thinking and their playing. We learned that the curriculum must be deep and broad, reflecting and responding to new and varied interests which emerge from the children, supporting expansion into projects. Our plans for the children's time must extend beyond the day, beyond the week and sometimes for many weeks on end, to foster deeper understanding and work (like play, a 'process' richest without a built-in schedule or timer). See Part Five.

We learned that children have daily experience with materials and arts, called languages in the Reggio community, through which they can express and explore their ideas and feelings. They will come to understand that they have approval and permission to explore these materials/languages, and discover their possibilities. As they become familiar with them, they use them to express what they want to say and they grow in craft and comfort. Ideally there will be an *atelierista* – a studio artist[4] – on your program's staff to support and assist teachers and children. This is Part Six of the book.

---

4. See Materials Chapters for more information about the *atelierista*.

A note about Reggio Emilia

It's a city of about 130,000 in prosperous Northern Italy, a study in contrasts – a large Catholic community, a Communist government, a Lamborghini Factory, and it's the source of wonderful Parmigiano-Reggiano cheese. It is an ancient, beautiful city, and one that has, in its best years, spent an amazing 17% of the municipal budget on the childcare program we admire and which inspires this book.

In Reggio Emilia, school buildings are different, timing is different, staffing is different, evaluation mechanisms and motives for evaluating are different from ours. The commitment they hold most importantly is an Image of Children as powerful, competent, full, and possessed of enormous powers of expression and with agendas of their own which get the respect they fully deserve. The teachers, artists, and pedagogues who support the children in this work are challenged to always be alert to children's signals, and to be on the side of community's wholesome growth.

People visit Reggio Emilia from all over the world to see what the best work with children looks like, return home excited by the possibilities for children they've seen – and some try to duplicate what the Reggiani do. Our writing recognizes that North America is different from Northern Italy, and shares our experiences trying to make *here* something that is informed by what we saw *there*. Our findings necessarily suit *our* culture. Ideas and experiences stemming from Reggio provocations have profoundly changed our thinking about what should happen here in programs for young children, and we believe you will be intrigued and challenged by them too!

Instead of setting down prefabricated permanent answers, we must keep thinking and paying attention to what the children are doing and saying and showing us. Rules get us into trouble; we try not to end up with rules that don't make sense or don't work. Children need to think things through and to see us do the same.

In Reggio Emilia, opposing ideas are celebrated and explored. Intellectual difference, even conflict, is *expected*, and challenging others to explain their ideas when you don't understand or agree with them is anticipated and encouraged; Reggio teachers have solid thinking behind what they do, and they can tell you why they are doing it. They challenge us, saying: "In Reggio when we disagree – the conversation begins. In the U.S., when educators disagree – the conversation stops."

We have tried to write here only about things we have experienced, and in working out what to say we have had conversations in agreement and in disagreement. These conversations are not always easy, but we believe they are deeply rewarding, and we are glad to share them! We want this book to start many more of those conversations – and we welcome conversation with you, our readers. Our email addresses: *sydney@eceteacher.org*   *lesliegleim@yahoo.com*

PART I: IMAGE OF THE CHILD

A four-year old in my 1973 class made this exquisite self-portrait. Photo: SGC

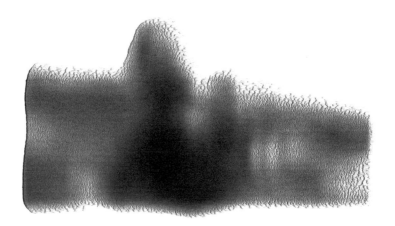

The Reggio Emilia Image of the Child

Carlina Rinaldi, pedagogista and Director of Early Childhood Services in Reggio Emilia[2] wrote this excellent summary of the Reggio Emilia Image of the Child:

> The cornerstone of our experience, based on practice, theory and research, is the image of the child as rich in resources, strong and competent, rather than simply needy. They have potential, plasticity, openness, the desire to grow, curiosity, a sense of wonder, and the desire to relate to other people and to communicate.
>
> Their need and desire to communicate and interact with others emerge at birth and are essential elements for survival and identification with the species. This probably explains why children are so eager to express themselves within the context of a plurality of symbolic languages, and why children are also very open to exchanges and reciprocity as deeds and acts of love that they not only want to receive but also want to offer. These form the basis of their ability to experience authentic growth . . . [3]

As we learn from Reggio Emilia while far away from Italy, we consciously develop our own "strong Image of the Child." "Strong" doesn't only describe the child's strength, but also indicates that the Image itself has to be strong, to overcome our own conventional thinking. Why must we undertake a process of change and then act on our changed awareness? Because we intend to give our children the best we can imagine, discover and offer. Let us begin by examining the old image.

The conventional Image of the Child

The nearsighted image we see all around us, framing most textbooks and curricula for children, says children are born empty, that they need to be filled up with information (mostly facts) so they can take on the work of the world. In college courses teachers are sometimes taught a child-centered curriculum but then they often find their job forces them into adult-focused instruction. There are pervasive messages in our society: babies and toddlers are to be stimulated and entertained (with bright primary colors, cartoons and noisy plastic toys), and preschool children need to be externally motivated or they'd

2. Carlina Rinaldi now fills the role originated by Dr. Loris Malaguzzi. See *page i* of this book.
3. Quoted in *The Hundred Languages of Children*, Edwards et al, Second ed. Page 114.

When we follow four-year-old Sally's lead, taking into account what our observations of Sally have told us about her, we learn more about her and how to be good resource people to her. When we insist that children follow our lead, we find that they frequently resist and subvert our plans, preferring instead to follow their own perfectly good plans.

Our *mindfulness* needs to increase. Sylvia Boorstein wrote: "Mindfulness is knowing what is happening in this moment and what is happening in me in response to it."

Mindfulness helps us strengthen our Image of the Child and that helps us to grow full-spectrum people.

How I began to develop my strong Image of the Child

When I started to teach I had good intentions and liked children, but I had the wrong instincts and had to learn my craft: to *lower* my voice if I wanted children's attention, to pay immediate attention to the child who was hurt instead of the one doing the hurting, to give children a lot of choice. As I learned better ways to work with children I became known as the most flexible teacher in the building, but that didn't interfere with my ability to assert my own authority as needed to keep the children safe, healthy, courteous to each other and engaged in activity that would benefit them later. My class was always the first group out of the building in a fire drill.

When I visited Reggio Emilia in 1992, what I saw there spoke to my most deeply held values and led me to a new understanding of teaching with integrity and authenticity. Somehow I've been lucky enough (possibly because of my own painful childhood) to stay sensitive to how children feel. I often get a deep message from children about their feelings and about how people — parents or other caregivers or teachers — support or dismiss their feelings.

Visiting Reggio Emilia I saw that the Reggiani were deeply sensitive to children's emotions, actions and explorations. When Dr. Malaguzzi told us that the foundation of their work was their Image of the Child as rich, competent, full, and more, I began to see that this idea, this strong Image, would unify many of the things I had already learned — not to talk about children in front of them as if they didn't matter, not to threaten children in order to get them to work, not to prohibit things they were already doing capably such as climbing high on a fence or hillside. I realized that I now had to listen to the children in a fresh way, and to observe them differently, looking and listening to see and hear what they *could* do, *wanted* to do, what *they* had in mind.

heard people say they respect the children yet speak about them as if they weren't sensitive. I've heard adults forbid a child to do something she has done successfully many times and *knows she can do well*. This kind of (pervasive) disrespect for children distorts, confuses and clouds our observations.

Nina challenged my Image of the Child during one very long moment. One weekend we reorganized the classroom. Our newly arranged space featured many transparent containers, some of them made of glass, holding both familiar and new materials. When the children arrived Monday our rearranged room surprised them.

Nina, a child with cerebral palsy affecting her coordination and her walking, began to make her way over to the shelves. Walking was always a struggle for Nina, so it was great to see her wanting the gorgeous stuff enough to make the arduous journey. She arrived at the shelves and examined each container. I held my breath watching her reach for a crystal cup filled with beads. After a struggle, she grasped the cup and was able to cradle it. She looked thrilled — and I panicked; had I been crazy to put out all this glass?

Nina worked the glass against her chest and walked back to the table. I restrained my urge to get the glass and carry it for her — after all, she was a four-year-old with cerebral palsy! Nina had been my student for many months and knew I would help her if she asked, but she didn't ask. My inner voice, newly informed by readings from Reggio Emilia, asked, sternly, "Do you *truly* believe that *all* children are rich, full, and competent?" If this child didn't feel competent to take the glass cup to the table, she wouldn't be doing it. If I truly hold a strong Image of the child, if I believe in the confidence she displays, I have to bow to her judgment. If I am going to continue my journey with ideas from Reggio Emilia I have to *believe* in her competence.

She struggled with her first step, and continued slowly, awkwardly, to carry the glass cup to the table. As she reached the table she glanced over at me as if to say "I did it, I knew I could, thanks for trusting me, thanks for respecting me enough to not jump in and help me." And she smiled. As I observed and documented Nina my Image grew stronger and broader. As my new Image of the Child grew, the children, starting with Nina, lived up to it. ᒼᗩ᠑   Note: This symbol will be used throughout the book to indicate the end of Leslie's comment, and the resumption of Sydney's voice.

- Painting
- Clay work
- Wire
- Dramatic play (including dressing up)
- Collage
- Instrumental music
- Song
- Dance

In Reggio Emilia adults introduce children to a medium that can become a language after a child has explored it in depth and at length, a process I salute and call "messing about."6 Once the child has become comfortable in the language, she can use it to represent what she thinks. She has gone from the messing about stage to fluency in the new language. We've heard that "If you only have a hammer, everything looks like a nail." Reggio thinking suggests, "if you have only a hammer, you need more tools and we'll introduce you to them."

Negotiation benefits both child and adult

As children engage with materials and with each other they reveal to us possible directions for further exploration, providing us with the opportunity to develop authentic leadership and support. The dialogue between the child's intention and the teacher's resources is personal, timely, tailored to the particular child (or children), and enriches and educates both. As a bonus our new strong Image of the Child and our growing skills as responsive teachers mitigate the teacher burnout caused by inauthentic, rote, or unimaginative functioning. As time passes, instead of using only her pitching arm all day long, the teacher uses different muscles while the child is tossing the ball back. The traditional style of teaching was edu*taining*, with the teacher at the front of the room, showing children things they should want to learn. The practice we learn from the Reggiani is edu*cating*, bringing out resources that the children can use to construct knowledge.

Those who attempt to understand and implement the Reggio Emilia Approach are upholding a long humanist tradition that cultivates critical thinking, exploration and research, and honors childhood's amazing wonderings. How very much this contrasts with the current fashion (2011) in the United

---

6. This wonderful term comes to us from the British Infant School movement of the 1960s, a remarkable and widespread experiment in allowing young children's choices to be central in their education. See Weber and also Plowden in bibliography.

respond more profoundly. New languages, materials and surprises provoke new thinking.

Observation helps a teacher explore the *meaning and function* of play for a child, so the teacher can develop questions or *provocations* to determine what will be needed to extend and deepen the play. When we are too hasty and immediately rush to extend play we run the risk of overwhelming children's thoughts, ideas or plans, stifling the very thinking we mean to encourage! One colleague says: "So many times I have, in my hurry, missed the children's point when they are really asking me to let them tell me what they know." The documentation process[9] guides us toward a more mindful, accurately targeted response which has far greater potential to fulfill the child's intention than an instant reaction does.

When might you want to provoke children in this way? When a child has shown you a general area of interest, you look for the precise part of that interest — the hot part — that matters to the child.

Sometimes after you've observed the children and talked with your colleagues, no further provocation is needed, but even consideration of possible provocations can assist you in planning.

Life provokes. Five-year-old Anthony's water experience was limited to showers and wading pools, so when I took him to a swimming pool, he began to think about going into water in a new way. A year later I drove Anthony across the George Washington Bridge. From the car, he noticed the Hudson River beneath us — and exclaimed, "That's a *big* swimming pool!" Traveling outside of his neighborhood had provoked him and made his thinking change, as travel so often does. If finding out about Reggio work has made you think that you've been teaching children in a superficial way, learning to provoke their thinking will help your teaching become more profound. A good start is to consider the question: "How am I going to introduce this subject so it will be most productive?" The resulting provocation is what you'll use to help yourself and the children enter deeper waters.

In one Reggio project the first substantial provocation was to have children compare drawings they made today with verbal descriptions they made yesterday, and notice which was a clearer description of what happened. Then the children considered why the drawings were inadequate, and listed what drawing skills they needed to learn, in order to show what they had described. This provocation set up a curriculum for weeks!

---

9. The subject of Part Two, The Documentation Process.

"programmazione" (programming) and the expressive, investigatory goals "progettazione" (pro-ject'-ing), and they choose to spend their time and energy exploring and following the possibilities of the latter. You will read more about this in our chapter on Projects.

Don't answer too quickly

In the story that became the title of my first book, *The Sun's Not Broken, A Cloud's Just in the Way: On Child-Centered Teaching,*[11] Hamid asked me, "The sun's broken?" during a long spell of dark, foggy weather. I told Hamid "It feels that way, Hamid, but the sun's not broken, a cloud's just in the way." He went away, seemingly satisfied. Now, as I reflect on it, I realize that when we (kindly and helpfully but forgetting our new strong Image of the Child) supply this kind of answer, we end the discussion just as I did, unfortunately, at that time. I didn't facilitate an opportunity for Hamid to construct his understanding — his own theory of weather changes — and I should have.

As adults begin learning to follow a child's lead and then to provide provocations and resources, we tend to head straight to solutions (the way I did with Hamid). Initially, we don't know how to *probe* for the children's deeper meanings. Our adult listening skills still have to be developed. We haven't yet learned how best to reflect the question back to the children, to *begin* a dialogue, instead of shutting it down. Knowing what I know now, I could have told Hamid, "It sure *feels* broken. Let me think about that, and you think about it too, and we'll talk again later." I'd have written down, in front of Hamid, a note to myself to come back to him with some ideas about finding out why the sun felt broken. He was using the metaphor of machines breaking down, a familiar metaphor in his community. Tossing the ball back, I could have helped him explore ways things disappear besides being broken — for example, hidden behind a curtain, or tucked inside a bag. Then he could move in the direction of constructing *another theory*, one based on nature rather than machines.[12] Re-opening the discussion after we'd both had time to think would have resulted in a very different journey for us.

---

11. The book, published by Gryphon House, is out-of-print at this time. You can often find inexpensive copies at abebooks.com or e-mail me at *sydney@eceteacher.org* I try to have some copies on hand.
12. See *page 51*

---

full and rapt attention. In the third photo the caregiver holds the watch to the baby's ear, letting her hear the tick-tock. (The modern reader must remember this was in the '80s, before digital, silent watches came into use.)

When I show these photos to a workshop group, I stop here, and ask the participants to each tell another person what will happen next. I promise that it's the next logical thing to happen. After they've had time to share their theories with each other, I show them the last photo. The baby has her ear to the magazine, *checking to see if these watches also tick-tock.*

My audience's energy is always electric at this moment. Most of the people present don't figure it out until I show the last photo to them. People who predicted things like "she'll put the watch in her mouth" or "the baby will wear the watch" realize that they have grossly underestimated Laura who, at age 12 months, has *made and tested an hypothesis.* "If that one ticks," Laura thinks, "perhaps the ones printed on the page will tock too?" And she listens, to check her hypothesis!

After the group has seen all four photos, just about everyone is thrilled at Laura's highly intelligent analysis. As Henry David Thoreau said, "It's not what you look at that matters, it's what you see." Those who expect the watch to go into Laura's mouth often insist "but that's the stage this baby is at" as if that was adequate justification for what they thought. Finally, many people promise themselves to see children more clearly, as individuals, not only as representatives of their age group.

I want them to find out about Laura from Laura *herself,* instead of depending on *generalized knowledge* about her stage of life, learned from a textbook. We must respect and attend to the child in front of us, and never depend solely on abstractions or generalizations. The documentation process (see Part Two) guides us toward a more mindful, targeted response that has greater potential to fulfill the child's intention than any *instant, immediate reaction* could.

Our goal is to help children's work continue and deepen. We want the children's play to become more complex, we want the children to experience investigating and creating things that take time and thought. As we look for ways to support this process we will become more careful listeners. As the children's play deepens, when they are encouraged and empowered to explore their theories and ideas, we adults also grow in our ability to understand and support the ways the children think; how they process and work through theories, ideas, and projects. Meanwhile the children's understanding and appreciation of *their own capability* increases. The key question is: how do we

CHAPTER 2
One ball at a time
By Leslie Gleim

Here's an important experience, showing Leslie's developing Image of the Child and how it helped her connect to a little boy. The other adults in the school — who had a weak image of the child — thought him beyond help.

Everyone had given up on Justin, an almost-5-year-old in the class down the hall. When Justin arrived at our school he could speak in short phrases but generally used only a word or two. Instead of talking, he bit children and adults daily in a way that seemed intentional, unpredictable, and savage. Other children complained when he came near them, fearful of his hitting, biting and pushing. Although Justin wasn't in my class, I observed him and wondered if some of the reactions of the teachers — putting him in "time out," scolding him for his misbehavior, and seldom acknowledging his good behaviors — were making him misbehave even more.

When that school year ended I volunteered to have him in my class. The school's director and I both felt that if ever a child needed our special approach, Justin was that child. My journal for that year shows not only Justin's journey but also my own. My work helped me rid myself of old attitudes and solidify my Image of the Child so I could understand what was happening and help Justin.

My Image of the Child is tested

From his first day with us I saw that Justin needed me far more than the other children in our group. Our first month together confused and perplexed me — never before had I encountered a child like this. His biting, hitting and shoving seemed to be random, unprovoked. By now all the other teachers

10/13. More questions: What do we consider "normal" behavior? Who is the judge? What right does this school have to create a different standard for Justin? What tools does Justin need so he can learn with and from his peers? How can the other children help him? What can I do to support peer assistance and to give Justin new ways to cope? I have observed so much of Justin's positive behavior during the past two months! I've seen him wait patiently for a turn, work gently beside other children building with clay, drawing side by side on the chalkboard with classmates Alyssa and Ethan, stooping down to pick up a toy and then handing it to Timmy, our youngest child. These golden moments let me see that he wants to belong to this community. How can we support him?

10/16. Today, after the first shift of children went home, I went outside with Sara, Andrew, and Justin. All three children headed for the tricycles. Later, Andrew stopped riding and began walking on the ledge of the large flower box framed with wide landscaping timbers. Andrew walked as if it were a tightrope. Soon Sara joined him. Justin stopped riding his tricycle and watched them. I asked Justin, "Can you do what Andrew and Sara are doing?" He said "Sure," and jumped up on the ledge and joined them. Then all three children pranced on, teetering back and forth, arms out for balance as they walked along the ledge.

Soon all three were giggling and laughing. Justin was happy. He laughed out loud. Not only was he happy with himself, he was included in the community of these other two children! The moment was enchanting!

Next Justin asked me to come and play with them. I joined in their play. After a few moments I pretended I was going to fall and said, "I need help!" Justin, from in front of me, said, "Here! Hold on." Astonished, and a bit cautious — because previously he hadn't liked anybody to touch him from behind and had bitten them for doing it — I put my hands on his shoulders. Now he said, "Hold on tight, Teacher." We worked our way around the flower box — First Sara, then Andrew, and then Justin with me holding onto him. We laughed and laughed. On one of our circuits I glanced over and saw an orange ball from the ball pit lying on the sidewalk! It reminded me not to hurry this child, to remove only one ball at a time, to let Justin emerge at a gentle pace.

The buses arrived to take the children home, so our playing had to end. The children gathered their backpacks and walked ahead. I asked Justin to wait for me since he tended to run alarmingly and I put out my hand for him to

The doctors said that it would take forty-five minutes or so after each seizure for Justin to recover. With this information I was able to begin to separate him from the other children so he wouldn't get anxious and defensive, and so that nobody would be hurt.

The doctor took my observations and notes into consideration as he determined Justin's daily medicine dosage. On certain days, before correct dosages were established, or when his medicine hadn't been administered, he'd have a storm of seizures. Matters were complicated by Justin's mother who, at first, was not disciplined enough to give him his medicine every day. On the days when he obviously wasn't medicated, I made it a practice to call her, insisting that she come and get him, telling her the medicine wasn't working. This tactic worked, and soon she learned to give Justin his medicine on schedule.

After his medicine dosage was stabilized, Justin's days at school became seizure-free. A new Justin emerged. Now he was able to enjoy school without frightening himself or others or missing parts of his day. His outbursts and anger began to disappear. Justin made friends with other children. As his seizures came under control his smile warmed us every day, and the smiles and giggles that first appeared on the flowerbox ledge that riveting day in October now warmed our January.

2/14. We were in the middle of a staff meeting when Justin and his Mom came in. His Mom said, "Sorry to interrupt your meeting, but Justin and I were at the store and he found this." She held up a ceramic valentine bear that said "I love you." "Justin insisted that I get it for Teacher. He wouldn't let me go home until we stopped by here and gave it to you." Justin brought me the bear, smiling from ear to ear. Then he threw his arms around me and hugged me!

This was Justin's thank you. He had inspired and challenged me to observe him closely enough to find the cause of his distress, to become a fighter on his behalf, and to let go of the remaining vestiges of the Behavior Modification-based teaching I was trained in. Learning how to allow Justin, untroubled, to emerge, I finally and fully embraced the Image of a strong, powerful, capable Child.

9/2006 (4 years later) Reviewing the documentation of my journey with Justin revealed my own growth as a teacher during that year.

CHAPTER 3
Get clear about why you do what you do

Once upon a time, a woman phoned her husband and asked him to "Stop at the butcher shop on the way home, buy a pot roast, and have the butcher cut off five inches from the end." The husband, in a hurry, said he'd do so, and hung up.

When he arrived home with the meat in a brown paper bag, the husband asked his wife "why cut off the five inches?"

The wife said, "I don't know. My mother always had the butcher cut off five inches, so I do, too."

They telephoned Mom, and asked her why the five inches were to be cut off. Mom replied, "I don't know. My mother always had the butcher cut off five inches, so I do, too."

So they telephoned Grandma, and asked her. "Simple, "she replied. "My pot was too short."

This traditional story illustrates a fundamental educational principle: ***don't do anything in your classroom unless you understand why you're doing it.*** Many things not worth the children's time have been *handed down* as early childhood rituals. I'm going to call them pot roast.

Our new image of the child doesn't permit pot roast! Here's Leslie's experience:

The rigid schedule (biggest pot roast of all)

For many years I felt constrained by the schedule on the wall — our day was controlled by the schedule:

We also had to coordinate our times with the private childcare program housed in our building and with the staff who tended to the yard. We adults learned to check in with each other, sharing our sense of when the children were ready to move on. We had abandoned the rigid institutional schedule, moving to our own, *tailored-to-fit,* rhythm!

When they enter in the morning, as they greet each other, some children survey the room for any surprises they may find. Other children browse the documentation area to see photos of work they've done and still others go watch the computer scrolling through images from yesterday. Some other children go directly to the block area, the easel or the play house, diving into work they've planned on their way to school.

The chunks of a recent day turned out to be:

8:00-10:15   Arrival, time in large motor room, transition when we were ready to our room for breakfast and children's choice of activity

10:15-11:15   Some children in a small group learning encounter, developed in response to teacher observation of children. *The other children are working with activities of their own choosing.* Teachers stay aware of IEP (Individual Education Plan) goals and make sure they're included in this small group work. Now, instead of automatically rotating every half hour, we stayed the full time in one activity classroom. Additionally, each class had a home room (mine was the Art Room) where they spent most of each day. Toileting, as needed.

11:15-12:00   Washing hands and lunch in the lunchroom.

12:00-12:45   Work with continuing activity or new provocation, in our room. This would be the teacher's choice. Sometimes some children went elsewhere with an aide while Leslie worked with a group on a particular project.

12:45-1:30   Some children nap, others are outdoors when weather permits or in gym

1:30-2:15   Toileting, washing hands, and snacks

2:15 – 2:30   Gym or outdoors, prepare to go home, schoolbus or parents pick up children.

This was the printed schedule. In reality we adjusted times and the amount of time spent in each block varied according to the children's level of engagement.

didn't like. I've seen teachers and parents start to count — and the counting sounds ominous. I've seen them tell children they won't be allowed to — go outdoors, have dessert, watch TV or videos, go on the field trip, play with the toy — and then seen the teacher either *carry out* such a threat or *forget* it. I'm not sure which is worse for the children.

In Reggio Emilia adults are alert to surprising behaviors and find them *interesting*. Reggiani think creatively about why the child does this thing, knowing that *behavior has reasons*. They bring past experience forward to inform the present situation, *looking closely at what is different in the new situation*.[18] They call this *"problematization"*[19]. We've seen how Leslie approached and later revised her schedule when she realized it was pot roast. When teachers and parents slow down and analyze each bothersome situation, they are more likely to find satisfactory solutions, and less likely to burn out.

Our job requirements often impede developing a strong Image of the Child. We sometimes whistle tunes that aren't so happy, to satisfy insurance requirements or administrators or politicians — people who usually don't know our children and cannot see how their rules wreak havoc in our lives. They impose standards and leave us to fulfill them. It's frustrating to be barred by bureaucracy in this way, and kept from using possible resources. Our new Image of the Child means following the children's lead. Leslie found that we incidentally meet those standards while we primarily concentrate on *meeting children's needs*.[20]

Leslie, in the Daily Sheets she provided to parents early in her Reggio journey, indicated how the Ohio State Standards were being met. She didn't have to add activities to meet those standards, just to keep her eye on the activities of the children and then list how those standard items were covered in the natural course of events. We must never shift the curriculum away from the children's interests and well-being to meet the needs of a faceless external imposer of standards.

Let the children practice! You already know how

Ask yourself: Is there something I do or announce every day that some of the children have learned? If so, relinquish those tasks to a child, or rotate them among volunteering children. This can be "we have to be quiet when

---

18. For a longer discussion of "Reading Behavior" see Clemens, S. *Pay Attention to the Children, Lessons for Teachers and Parents from Sylvia Ashton-Warner,* pp 132-135.

19. See *page 128.*

20. We're not against standards, but expect that they should vary with the individual, so the standards a professional musician meets are different from those required of a carpenter, and of the amateur musician, as well. The same goes for children. One standard for all seems to create ice cube trays — though all children are unique!

Instead, the senior teacher said to me, in a kind voice while patting me sympathetically on the hand, "Perhaps you haven't worked with this age group — you will want to know that they don't do representational drawing."

I replied, "Yes, but when children can't talk we still talk with them, *expecting* that they will grow into conversation. I think it's the same way with drawing."

I expected a defensive response, but I was wrong. The teacher's eyes opened wide, and she said, "I must have been doing my job too long. I've gone on automatic!" I was awed by her response, and told her so. I continued to observe and meet with teachers in this center for the next day-and-a-half, but this incident burned brightly in my mind. At our closing meeting, after each person present listed one thing she or he had learned, I retold this story, and said it reminded me of a grave danger in our work. Then I told them the Pot Roast Story.

The sad part of being a consultant is that often I fly in and teach and then I fly out having little or no idea afterwards what anyone found useful. Imagine my delight months later when center director Pam Boulton let me know that her staff had decided to have a monthly Pot Roast Meeting, for the purpose of examining existing practices to see if they were happening because they were habit, (in which case they would be discarded) or because the present context *warranted* them.

Years later, I wrote to Pam, asking what had become of their pot roast meetings. Here's her reply:

> We haven't had any actual pot roast meetings for quite a while, but the phrase often comes up — and as we explain to newer staff what we mean, the conversations start spontaneously. It has now become part of the culture.
>
> Sometimes we bring it up deliberately around a topic we are struggling with. Sometimes we simply ask a quick question about something — like "is this pot roast, or do we really need it to be this way?" It never fails to lighten the load with a laugh and it always brings good problem-solving skills to the fore. Thanks!

I've been wondering, ever since, how to get other agencies to have such meetings. *Looking at what we always do — to see if we mean to be doing it now, with these children, in these circumstances — can free us from the past and make us more effective today and in the future, improving the services we offer our community.*

to learn to view each problem with a focus and emphasis on what the child can *already understand* and do, not what she is lacking — keeping your work authentic. The examples from Leslie's and Marie's classrooms in this book exemplify the way.

In North America many of our communities are multicultural, in contrast to Reggio Emilia where nearly all of the people are Italian by heritage, birth and culture.[23] Here, where a wide variety of cultures mix together, there are more chances for cultural misperceptions and colliding values, and these differences must be considered and discussed as part of the general understanding of their community by teachers and parents. Furthermore, a wider range of educational levels exists here. Our rich are richer and our poor are poorer also making any dialogue more complex. Admittedly, the clash of various cultural values is a complicated discussion, but to ignore or avoid it is to bury these real differences and promote *mis*understanding. As a multicultural democracy, we strive for *all* voices to enter into the conversation, for *all* voices to be heard.[24]

Learning to change the way you think about the Image of the Child

A colleague on the Reggio online discussion group challenged:

Everything I read on Reggio says, "It starts with the Image of the Child," so why do we still have children who can't initiate play, never mind sustain play? Children who have tantrums when they don't get their way? I've even got a child, Mary Jean, who still bites at age four years six months. What about a child who falls off chairs when she is sitting on chairs — never mind letting her stand on them?"

Here's Leslie's reply:

By the time Mary Jean has reached four years six months she has chosen many strategies and developed many theories about how to make the world work. Some of her choices are good, and some — including the ones you list — aren't. But what is clear is that the child is the one making theories and choosing strategies.

It's very easy to view Mary Jean as strong and competent when she is playing nicely, running well, speaking clearly and listening closely to what's being

---

23. This situation is changing as more and more people migrate into the Reggio Emilia area, and it will be interesting to see how the Reggiani deal with newcomers and their children.
24. See Patricia M. Cooper's excellent book, *The Classrooms all Young Children Need,* about the work of Vivian Gussin Paley. 2009 University of Chicago Press, especially Chapter 5, Race, "Pedagogy, and the Search for Fairness."

child and our positive Image of her. When we do this, we provide children real support.

We believe the Mary Jean behaves as well as she presently can, responding with strategies that seem to her to have worked in the past. If her strategies trouble us or trouble other children, we want to *enlarge the range of alternatives from which our competent child may choose.* We tell a child, "If you hit other children they will not want to play with you. *Tell them* when you don't like something, and they will listen." The child may not integrate or act upon this new information immediately, and the others may not always live up to our promise about them, but eventually she will learn to use it to modify her own behavior, because it will help her make friends and be part of our community.

Listen to children to refine your Image of the Child

As we learn to listen to children, we know we want to adopt something similar to the Reggiani's belief that children are born strong, competent, full, and more.

It takes time and work to change this fundamental orientation. Change is difficult!

Trying to make ourselves find a way to believe in the strong Image, we practice the new idea, just as Anna, in *The King and I*, practices being unafraid:

> *I whistle a happy tune*
> *And every single time*
> *The happiness in the tune*
> *Convinces me that I'm not afraid!* [25]

Helen Dion,[26] a teacher, similarly reports:

> *When a child tells me "I can't do it"*
> *I find myself telling him or her "pretend you can."*
> *They do, and they do it!*

---

25. Lyric from *The King and I*, by Oscar Hammerstein II.
26. on the Reggio online discussion group, 2000.

CHAPTER 4
Intention and moral pain

I reach a hand into the mind of the child, bring out a handful of the stuff I find there, and use that as our first working material. Whether it is good or bad stuff, violent or placid stuff, coloured or dun. To effect an unbroken beginning.
— *Sylvia Ashton-Warner*

A child flourishes when she expands the range of her understandings and ability to solve the problems that interest her. Perhaps the hardest task adults must accomplish, when learning to think in Reggio terms, is to *uncover, find and follow the intention of the child.* Babies know when they are uncomfortable, and call us to feed, clean, and assist them or allow them to fall asleep. After a while adults want to add their own times and ideas to those of the baby, and if the adults are sensitive, harmony results. Unfortunately, sometimes adults *take over,* ignore the child's signals, substitute their own needs, schedules and wishes, and create frustration and imbalance.

If older infants and children seem ready to play, we're doing well when we initiate play and then go forward if it's well received, or quickly abandon it if the child's not interested. If we plunge forward only because we have the time or the inclination to play — regardless of how this idea is received by the child — our message has become: *I know better than you do,* or *my ideas are more important than yours.* Humans, including babies, generally don't like this message.

Similarly, despite what everybody thinks, when adults say "children have short attention spans" they are talking about children *who are being asked to attend to things chosen by adults.* A two-year-old on a beach with a pail and shovel lives in joy, outside of time. He will play in the sand with or without

The image of the teacher

Our new understanding of children means we need to redefine the role of the adult, no longer primarily a transmitter of information — we'll never be as good at that as search engines are. The teacher is no longer the star performer in the classroom, but *instead a facilitator of caring and mindful relationships not only between people, but also between things, between thoughts, and with the environment.* We teachers must see ourselves as researchers and facilitators: able to think, analyze and produce a true curriculum, a curriculum emerging from our own gifts and those of the children. We must not continuously impose adult intentions on the children — impeding them from following their interests and working in their own way — but instead allow children to proceed, creating their theories and testing them, with our help as needed.

No matter how new you may be to teaching, and whether you work with an atelierista or some other collaborator to help you explore children's intentions and theories for their next steps and possible projects, it's crucial that you know what you're asking of children, and that you're clear about how a good classroom climate feels, looks and sounds. When the environment is supportive, comfortable and safe the children can more easily identify their intentions and then find the courage to reveal those intentions to adults. That brings us to the moment when we can be of assistance.

Discovering the children's intention isn't easy — often the children themselves are unclear about what they want or insufficiently articulate to explain it. We have to be patient and respectfully restrained as a child struggles with half-formed ideas, limited vocabulary or immature pronunciation to help us understand what he or she wants. Initial expression of interest in one thing may cloak another.[29]

Emotions

We can see, in the projects with three- to six-year-olds the Reggiani have shared with us in their exhibits, talks, videos and publications, that the children are usually driven by strong feelings. In the case of *To Make a Portrait of a Lion,*[30] the children are awed by the king of the beasts, and love his power, his claws and his jaw. In another project[31] the children love the possibility of playing with their shadows, to make them grow or shrink, to try to escape from them. In the *Amusement Park for the Birds*[32] the children shelter and

---

29. I learned a great deal about this from Pam Oken-Wright. See footnote *page 6.*
30. Video: *To Make a Portrait of a Lion,* 1957. Available from Reggio Children. *http://www.reggiochildren.org*
31. *Everything Has a Shadow Except Ants,* 1999. Available from Reggio Children.
32. Video: *Amusement Park for the Birds,* 1992. Available from Reggio Children.

---

details of the drawing didn't accurately depict what they had seen and described. The next months of their year were spent exploring how to draw profiles and people seen from above, how to deal with noses (experiments in clay and drawing), considerations of the individuals in a crowd, and many more adventures with demystification of crowds. The project ended with the boys making a crowd in clay — reinventing the assembly line as they worked! — and the girls making another crowd of paper people with a cloud of language overhead (like in comic strips.) You can see these pictures in the catalog of the One Hundred Languages of Children Exhibit, 2nd Edition.

These projects exemplify the care and attention to children's intention that supports a child's interest into weeks, and sometimes months, of exploration, representation, conversation and celebration, the general form of a Reggio Emilia project.

Collaboration

In Italy the atelierista collaborates with the classroom teachers to further the children's intentions by extending the children's ability to express themselves in visual languages: drawing, painting, clay work and any of the other hundred languages. Collaboration among adults stimulates much deeper thinking about children. We'll have a whole chapter on collaboration during the Documentation Process in this book.

Pain can limit our image

A woman who had taught young children over an eight-year period, repeatedly leaving the field and returning to it, came to study with me. When we considered the documentation she brought with her, I saw that her projects didn't come to glorious conclusions and celebrations, like those in Reggio Emilia. Hers were sometimes unsuccessful and trailed off, leaving me sad. We discussed how she chose projects, and what shapes they took, and I urged her to notice , in documentation from Italy, that *Reggio projects end with a celebration.*

She defended: "Well, what we do in life doesn't always turn out that great." When I probed, she was adamant that children didn't always need their efforts to bear fruit — that the children had to be prepared for the disappointments of life. "I didn't have great outcomes as a child. I'm not sure I can give them to the children I teach, since I didn't experience them myself. I feel somewhat competitive with these children."

we're discussing. The Reggio community has been working on this difficult accomplishment since their schools began in 1945.[37] Our North American context is quite different, but optimism leads us to seek ways to cultivate a new, strong Image of the Child to benefit our children and our community.

As much as I could, from the beginning of my work as a teacher, I would search for ways to change things so as to make my Moral Pain go away. If I found myself fussing at the children before lunch (I don't like to think of myself fussing at children) I changed what we did at that time to something children liked better — of course, it worked! My friends who are still teaching in public schools under the restrictions of No Child Left Behind and Race to the Top are asked to do many things each day (prepare children for tests, emphasize phonics instead of understanding texts, and more) that they feel are wrong for children and themselves. Their Moral Pain is enormous.

As learners we struggle to acknowledge the gulf between *what I know is right* and *what I do,* and then to reduce that gulf. An inch closer, a mile closer — the closer the better — how great a change I can afford to make depends on my situation.

Examine your present life circumstances. For example: If you're a single parent and not independently wealthy, you can't afford to lose or risk your job. You know where the boundary is, and you don't dare to cross it now, so you will need to compromise, once or repeatedly — yet *always remember to call it a compromise.* You must *always* file these under "C" for Compromises and never under "R" for Right. It is possible that there will come a day when your children are grown, and you have a measure of security, when opportunity and circumstance will allow you to do what you believe in. You must always keep yourself ready to move to what you know to be right. In the meantime, *double track,* do what you have to do now, while thinking: "If I had the freedom I deserve and used it well, how would I *choose* to do this?"

You're in danger if you find yourself moving from "I don't believe in that," to "It's all right because I have to do it to keep my job." You will want to remember a choice you made *against* your beliefs, and that your choice was a compromise. Otherwise, *what had been a painful choice becomes standardized, justified and unquestioned.* We must not allow this creeping legitimatization of compromises. You're on solid ground if you persevere in telling yourself, "I am compromising. This is the best I can do right now. I'll keep searching for a way to end this compromise, as my life continues and changes. (Have I inherited money? Is my significant other making enough money so I can now

---

37. There is also a Roman Catholic childcare program in Reggio Emilia, with a different culture, but not part of this discussion.

Children arrange flowers as an art activity at Okemos Nursery School School. Photo: Renae Slaton

CHAPTER 5
Integrated learning

UNESCO[38] reviewed early childhood policies and practices in developed countries.[39] Two of their observations strongly remind us of beliefs held in Reggio Emilia:

- The quality and effectiveness of programs do not depend entirely on wealth — some rich countries have poor systems and services — but on *the vision* that a country has for its children, backed by sound government planning, financing, and policy-making.

- There is a temptation to turn early childhood services into junior schools. Preparation for school is necessary, but research shows that *didactic classrooms* do *not* support effectively the *holistic development* of young children, in particular *their creative capacities,* and their *socio-emotional* and *physical development.*

Our Image of the Child is reflected in the questions that we pose, in our choices of materials, how we frame our day, our interactions with parents and in the design of our classroom and outdoor environments.

In this country children are seen as consumers from birth. Their environment has been distorted by over-stimulating, branded, commercial interests. There are many examples, Disney™ and other licensed characters and logos, which disfigure walls, rugs, backpacks, lunch boxes, tee shirts and notebooks. The children's world is cheapened by ugly, jazzy letters or numbers or animals or anything salable and yet deemed instructive. A deluge of commercials

---

38. *http://en.unesco.org/*
39. UNESCO Policy Brief on Early Childhood #26, Bennett, John. Curriculum in Early Childhood Education and Care September 2004.

Daryl, who had just had his fifth birthday a week before, wasn't happy with the letters in the word *Days* — three of those letters were too invasively close to his *own* name, his own special letters. Seeing his letters used differently disturbed him. We discussed this briefly, and I said something grownup and placating about how the same letters get used over and over many times in many different words.

We read and joked and learned the poem, and then I said "But Daryl, we weren't on acres of *ground,* you know, we were on. . ."

"Sand," he chirped.

I said, "Let's change the poem to say 'Acres of sand'". He agreed, so I got a pen and crossed out *ground* and wrote *sand.* Then he said, "Grandma, let's change this," as he pointed to Days, the word that had misappropriated his letters. "Let's make it say Kite Spring."

Then we went to the computer and fixed the whole thing up. And that's how Daryl learned to edit, learned that text was changeable! Just as I wanted the poem to reflect our reality at the beach, he didn't want his letters usurped, so we changed the text, making it work for us both!

KITE SPRING

By Mark Sawyer

Revised by Daryl Carl Dancy & Sydney Gurewitz Clemens

A kite, a sky,
And a good firm breeze,
Acres of sand
away from trees,
One hundred yards
Of clean, strong string
O boy, o boy!
I call that Spring!

We do well to use children's intense feelings to fuel their explorations and expression![40]

---

40. The story about Daryl and kites was first published in a slightly different form in *Early Childhood Research and Practice*, Volume 1, Number 1, as part of an article called "Editing: Permission to Start Wrong" *http://ecrp.uiuc.edu/v1n1/clemens.html*

fifth row, drawing the eye to the left. The top row, starting with recognizable flowers or trees, becomes more and more abstract; the progression is sophisticated. In the drawing below we see another set of messages going across the paper. These children are practicing to be writers, not because they're under pressure from the adults at their school, but because being able to write gives you power!

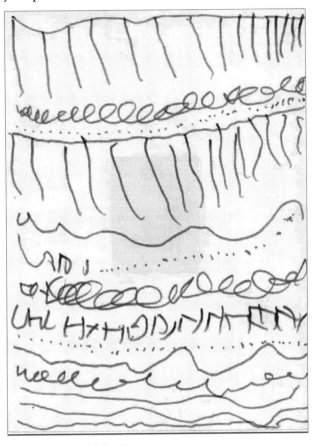

Deborah's second drawing

These children drew patterns (we can discern no words) just letters, numerals, and symbols, organized in lines the way they are in books, even using different fonts! In Reggio classrooms, the children's names are all displayed in lists (with photos) so children can look up their own names, as well as those of their classmates, and as part of a system of *mailboxes* where one can leave a small gift or picture for a classmate or teacher.

On the reverse side of his scary drawing, Matteo dedicated it to me. He was the only four-year-old who did, although many wrote their names, including Filippo, but not Deborah. Here is Matteo's writing:

The back of Matteo's drawing

I was also given pictures with writing on the reverse by the fives.

Here's a taste:

Daniele's drawing

Daniele was copying my name from my business card. He also copied my zip code!

CHAPTER 6
Interlude: Two small lessons from Vygotsky

LOVE THE QUESTIONS

I want to beg you as much as I can…
to be patient toward all that is unsolved in your heart
and to try to love the questions themselves…
Do not now seek answers which cannot be given you
because you would not be able to live them.
And the point is to live everything.
Live the questions now.
Perhaps you will then gradually, without noticing it,
live along some distant day into the answer.

— Ranier Marie Rilke
From *Letters to a Young Poet*

Lesson one: Vygotsky and Velcro™
Experience must be present for the learner to integrate new information

Vygotsky teaches us that experience needs to be present for *new information* to connect and hold. I like to use the image of Velcro,™ consisting of two parts, hooks and loops — which, when joined together create a strong bond. Vygotsky teaches us that *experience* (the loops) needs to connect with *new information* (the hooks) for learning to take place.

A child who has not traveled and seen mountains cannot think of them as snowcapped or bare, as having a tree line or being used for skiing. If she has read books about mountains she may have an inkling of what they are, but nothing duplicates the real-life experience of walking and breathing in real mountains. The *experience* part of the Velcro™ is absent. There is nothing to

Lesson two:
The Zone of Proximal Development (ZPD)

Background: Before we'd heard of Vygotsky, whose work was suppressed during the years when he wrote it, Piaget told us that children couldn't learn things until the children were at the right stage, and that stages couldn't be forced to come sooner. This was unsettling to teachers since we like to proactively give a child something new, and not to wait until some ambiguous interval elapses.

Vygotsky's work (which is highly regarded in Reggio Emilia) agrees that stages are, as Piaget taught us, not to be hurried, but he pointed out there is a period — during each stage — when the child approaches the next stage and becomes able to *borrow expertise* from an adult or a more skilled peer, and use what is shared by this expert so that the child can more comfortably operate in the stage she's about to enter. Vygotsky called this readiness period in advance of a next developmental stage, "the zone of proximal development (ZPD)."[41] He wrote:

> The distance between the actual developmental level as determined by independent problem solving and the level of potential development as determined through problem solving under adult guidance, or in collaboration with more capable peers.

When his teacher sees Bobby struggling with a task he can't do alone, awareness of the Zone of Proximal Development encourages the teacher to ask Bobby questions or offer him examples and assistance, so as to empower and enable *his* learning. Thus, she builds a scaffold he can step out onto while he's making his discoveries.

The scaffold, the shared expertise from an adult or skilled peer, helps Bobby do things *with others* that he can't yet do *alone*. His teacher or more skilled peer fills in with focused questions, targeted guidance, or other resources so he can succeed at this task.

Dr. Malaguzzi taught us that openness to curriculum that responds to the ideas of the people in the room "goes to undermine the role of the teacher. It makes the role of the teacher more complex and more beautiful and the teacher can become more involved. It calls for a different kind of formation of teachers than we're used to in preservice teacher training."[42]

---

41. L.S. Vygotsky: *Mind in Society: Development of Higher Psychological Processes*, 1978 p. 86.
42. This quotation is from a draft I received at a workshop. It became the Child Care Information Exchange article: *Your Image of the Child: Where Teaching Begins* in the March, 1994 issue.

---

take on a task of the next stage. On the scaffold the child can borrow our skill (or, better, the skill of a classmate) and continue along in an area that interests her, despite being unready to manage this task alone.

I have always liked showing people how to do something, and Vygotsky gave me approval for that, helping me find new energy in my teaching.

What is the role of the Vygotskian early childhood teacher?

If we are to follow Dr. Malaguzzi's advice to abandon certainty — the idea that we already know what's there — then, liberated by Vygotsky's thinking, we will become great explorers, detectives and archeologists, trying to uncover what's really there. We look for the children's intentions, provide them a full spectrum of resources, and become architects and engineers (planners and designers) who find space and provisions for their designs and constructions. This truly helps them develop the dispositions and skills they need to get the results they want.

We learn from the children, from our colleagues and friends and from our whole community as we explore collaboratively, thinking about what the children's behavior might be telling us. We try *many* things, hoping that what we try will move us in the direction of helping the children with their intentions, and we will sometimes succeed. We will learn from our errors, and search, not for new certainties, but for new ways of *exploring and understanding*, leading to new ways of assisting capable, rich, thoughtful children's explorations.

Vygotsky has explained why Reggio works so well: connecting curriculum to the child who is present ensures that the loops and hooks will connect and the information and ideas that come up in this connected context will support the child's growth and development. As Nobel Laureate Henri Bergson said, "The eye sees only what the mind is prepared to comprehend."

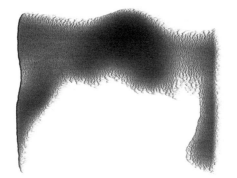

I watched and waited, ready for his next move. I believed the grin meant he was interested in what I had done. When he picked it up again and put it to his ear, I said, "Hello" again, and this time he replied, "Hello" before he put the phone down. I gasped in excitement, since this was the very first time this child had said a word I could understand!

He picked up his phone again. This time *he* said "Hello" *first*! I replied "Hello." Now he grinned and paused and mouthed something I couldn't understand. Then, with some difficulty, he said "Bye." Seeing my surprise Robert giggled and grinned, and then, with me following his lead, we repeated and repeated our hello and goodbye game. The children and I applauded, "Oh, Robert, you can talk!" ∾

Time to reflect

Information moves fast and disappears rapidly in an early childhood classroom. Part of learning to be a good observer is managing the rapid stream of information *to permit reflecting on our observations*. The documentation process is the tool which provides the structure and format for that learning. The next section of our book is about that process.

Dr. Malaguzzi tells us:

> Stand aside for a while and leave room for learning,
> observe carefully what children do, and then,
> if you have understood well,
> perhaps your teaching will be different from before.[46]

Through observing closely and being open to new possibilities, *by taking time to reflect on what we're doing*, we increase our own competence. *We must abandon the idea that we already know what is here.* What we know is *influenced, bounded and constrained by our past experiences*, and today's new experiences give us fresh data to process, and what we see this afternoon may challenge what we believed this morning. Thinking all the time takes work, but it sharpens and develops insight — something every good teacher needs.

---

46. In Edwards, Gandini & Forman, *One Hundred Languages of Children*, 1998.

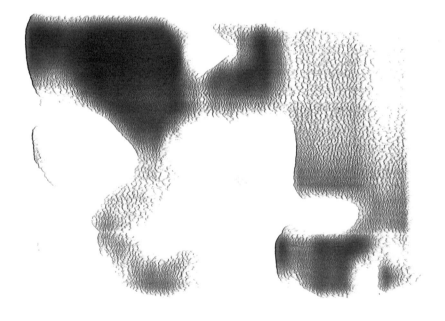

I sent some photos home with the children, and put some on the classroom walls, but, since I depend so much on words, I didn't realize yet *how much story could be told in pictures*. For many years my way of learning to understand children was to write down what they said and did — reviewing the day and planning the next with my assistant after the children went home.[47]

What did we write that grew us as teachers, before we'd heard the Reggiani's ideas about the documentation process? We wrote about the things that troubled us, trying to accurately describe behavior while avoiding judgment; leaving the guesses and theories until later, when we could review *all* the data we had collected, linking it with other information about a specific child to modify an old understanding or create a new perspective.

Sometimes we wrote down what children said — exactly the way they said it — including errors, confusions, cutenesses and even nonsense. We speculated about what all this meant, and included our theories and questions. I often wrote down what I *saw* when I couldn't hear the words (from across the school yard or across the classroom) looking carefully at what children did with their bodies, how they achieved satisfactions, whom they approached and how, and how they were treated by others when they approached them. Watching them I tried to educate myself about nonverbal communication and body language. I wrote about the way a child entered the classroom in the morning.[48] I wrote about whether the child went willingly or not if picked up before it was time to go home, and how the children greeted or ignored those who arrived, timely or late, at day's end to take them home.

Amazing things are recorded in my teaching journals. For instance, after five-year-old Marcie met my friend Tom *only once in January*, when he returned unannounced to help me with something in September, Marcie greeted him, casually, by name! More often we recorded the everyday miracles that happen as four-year-olds learn: when a child mastered the low-to-the-ground two-wheeler (amazingly, every year they all did!) or succeeded, after many tries, at tying her shoelaces. How the children cheered as we celebrated their friends' triumphs!

Media helps with our development

There are many ways to collect data: still or video camera, audio recorder, or simply writing on paper. Whatever media we use for collecting data, Leslie and I agree that using media supports reflection on our practice, and that *reflection* is what has improved and continues to improve us as teachers. Review

---

47. You can read more about logging in Clemens, *The Sun's Not Broken, A Cloud's Just in the Way.*
48. I came to believe that a kind, empathetic, perceptive greeting by an adult at the school could absolutely make a day better for a sensitive child. I learned a lot from Teacher Aide Katherine Primes, who knew exactly how to make a child and parent feel welcome on arrival.

CHAPTER 8
Changing the Image of the Child in this country

Children have wonderful ideas, often large, often intricate. What if, we ask, children were to hold on to those ideas, to believe that no matter how great or reaching the ideas, they could be made visible?

— *Pam Oken-Wright*

Since 2002, when the No Child Left Behind law was passed, American teachers have been mandated to follow scripts found in teacher's manuals that accompany textbooks, and to test children with standardized tests several times each year. Practically, this means teaching only the "official" text without veering from what is prescribed.[50] People in early childhood education (ECE) who teach in preschool programs are affected by the change in expectations of children about to enter Kindergarten, and people in ECE who teach kindergarten, first, or second grade are swept up in the mania for testing and pulled away from the real job, helping young children to grow and learn in ways that interest them and serve the community, to focus on "their creative capacities and their socio-emotional and physical development."

It will take lots of love and courage and political wit to induce our politicians to change these policies which utterly fail to acknowledge the uniqueness of each child. Our ability to effect this change will come as a result of looking with open hearts at children, parents and teachers, listening to them, and exchanging learning. Then we must find a way to convey changes that are needed to those who make policy. Action based on what our heightened consciousness and close observation show us will result in changes that benefit children and schools.

---

50. See the rigid *No Child Left Behind* legislation. And see Susan Ohanian's very informative webpage for ongoing critique of NCLB. *http://www.susanohanian.org*

even characters in novels or plays.) We learn and teach everything through *relationship*, and we do it best when the relationship is *trusting*. Only after you and I give each other some trust can we work well together.

With trust it is possible to discuss a difference and agree to explore it further, with each party listening closely and trying to bridge the gap, a kind of back and forth and zigzagging dialogue between two people with two perspectives. For example, a difference about the role of holidays in the school, about whether or not to have caps and gowns for preschool graduation, about phonics, school uniforms, school lunches, war play. That zigging and zagging, that examination and discussion of the range of alternative choices — the various routes to a destination — that's the 'dialectic' part. Each person explains his or her idea, and listens respectfully to the other's different ideas *and their reasons*. And in the process of talking and listening, they agree to differ and to disagree *without animosity*. And then they make a plan which, because of mutual respect, can succeed.

Successful engagement in this process is based on believing that you *both* want what's best for children, that your experience and truth and the other's are both valuable and worth considering. It's the realization and trust that complicated problems do not have simple solutions and that *you will still be friendly after the discussion*.

There's an old Yiddish expression, "In every argument, both sides are right." When all have listened and all have heard the many perspectives possible, the decisions we forge, together, are stronger than those that result from a power struggle.

Why do the Reggiani have this trust? Why do so many of us lack it? Every difference — race, class, nationality, gender — can either stimulate this kind of negotiation or stifle it. We have different histories and appearances, we have different styles and gifts. We're okay if the other person still recognizes what we have in common, knowing I am committed to children in most ways that matter to her. Similarly I know she is committed to the children in most ways that matter to me. We may diverge in detail or in method. When we discover a divergence, we are interested in it. The process can be difficult, but we explore to find something better for the children we care for. Mutual respect continues. Sometimes one of us modifies her opinion, sometimes both do, sometimes neither does, but with time the problem resolves, sometimes to where one or the other of us started, sometimes to a third alternative. Whatever the outcome, we find the *process* worthwhile. Neither of us needs to be defensive (and if defensive feelings arise we work through them). Excellent work is what matters, and we search for ways to accomplish it. As

Another colleague doesn't save documentation panels, or even her files, as if they were only for a single use, and wouldn't be helpful or informative later. Yet another colleague shares only baby steps in documentation, for fear colleagues will be overwhelmed. Another always leaps ahead to describe the desired outcome, instead of methodically noticing and sharing the steps along the path.

We cannot force others to accept the Image of the Child as the Reggiani present it to us. We can, however, keep on documenting children's many capabilities and strengths to others, hoping those resisting people will, sooner or later, become aware of the new Image and want to act on that new vision. We have a responsibility to share with our colleagues. Some will be envious, like the colleague I had who, at the end of each school year, would always ask me a version of the question: *"Sydney, how come you always get the good artists?"* She couldn't recognize that the children in my afternoon class hadn't come to the school as good artists, but had become good artists because we gave them *time to draw and paint and work in clay every day*, unlike her morning class where art was occasional and product-oriented.[52] Some of our colleagues will not think Reggio ideas worth the bother, but others will find them interesting, and begin their own journey.

Leslie writes about using documentation to help others "get it"

We can't spend time and energy worrying about changing others but we can hope that as others observe us and our work, their curiosity — about what it is that makes our children so very competent, so interested in life, so full of wonder and joy — may lead them in this new direction. Documentation panels[53] you make will influence people who read what you've posted to change their understanding and begin to shift their Image of the Child.

If I am in a leadership position with teachers who don't see, acknowledge and act based on children's competence, then I see my role as one of seeding and cultivating the environment with the questions that are raised through my documentation. I use the documentation process as a primary basis and resource for opening discussion with those who may want to learn about constructivism[54] and the Reggio Emilia Approach. I hope and believe that what we share will cause other teachers to be so uncomfortable that they will ask new questions of their own work. I see my role as projecting a passion

52. For detailed descriptions of my art program, go to my webpage: *www.eceteacher.org* and click "Articles, by me."
53. See Documentation, Part II of this book.
54. The idea that children must *build* their own understandings, that they cannot simply open up and let us drop understandings into them. The work of Jean Piaget, and later Lev Vygotsky, explains constructivism in depth.

observe the children more closely, and motivated me to connect more closely with the children's families, looking for the ideas and insights they could contribute to help me make a curriculum that honored children's potentials. When I first heard about Reggio in 1994 I felt this was the right journey for me.[56] I began to base my work on *what these children wanted to learn* and could learn, instead of what they were supposed to be trained to do.

A true curriculum

When I was teaching at Pacific Oaks College in the late 1980's I taught a class called "Emergent Curriculum." In recent years Leslie did a major project around preschool children doing much of their own planning, inventing graphics to represent their activities.[57]

We can revolutionize our teaching by transforming our individual and collaborative reflection, to harmonize with the children's innate *need to grow*. To do less is to rob ourselves and the children of many important and wonderful competencies all of us will need to confront the complex future.

Motivation: imposed or emergent? People like me, who went to teacher-preparation school in the 1960's and 1970's, were taught that every lesson plan had to have an objective and a motivation and the teacher was to write them down. Amazingly, the idea that the children were *already* motivated didn't arise! For people like us, changing our idea about the location of motivation was, itself, a big step, and had a domino effect, changing everything in our planning process as a result.

We're recommending a shift from external "motivations," from a pseudo-scientific approach, from the standardized, testing climate of No Child Left Behind and Race to the Top — to a tradition that comes from Plato, through Carl Jung, Herbert Read, and Nel Noddings. We want human sensitivity to inform the classroom. We want teachers to identify the *child's* motivations, and serve them, just the opposite of imposing a "Motivation" as part of a lesson plan.

If we teach children to read and write about what they care about, at the time they want or need the skill — the way they learned to speak — they will learn organically — the motivation will be theirs, not one imposed by another. Generally, a person learns best when he is motivated from *in*side.

---

56. At this time I began to read more and embrace new constructivist influences: Rheta DeVries, Constance Kamii, Lillian Katz, Gianni Rodari, David Elkind, and George Forman.
57. You can find information about this work and other projects Leslie has done at Mid-Pacific Institute in Hawai'i at: *www.midpac.edu/elementary/PG/archives.php*

We must face our scarred lives (we *all* have scars) and figure out how *not to pass along our emotional injuries to the children*. We need other adults, adults we trust, to help us stay balanced and honest. This new work is difficult, but it rewards us with the resilience we need for the hard work of teaching.

In the following story, Leslie's belief in a strong Image of the Child infects the child's mother.

How powerful is the Image of the Child I hold? Does it strengthen the faith that families of children with special needs have in their child's ability to grow and learn, only to have their new image of their child denied or violated once they leave our environment? I'm troubled by these questions when children move on to other schools, since the "big school" out in the real world, can treat a child with harsh and disrespectful indifference.

Merrylyn is a very bright child with Down Syndrome. In the four years she was in my class I did extensive documentation on her journey and learning. I watched her grow from using vague utterances and signs to speaking sentences, from scribbling to writing her name. Her very fine work has been recorded in several Videatives©.[61] When she was growing too old for our program a decision was made to send her to a separate Special Education unit. I refused to endorse this decision, since she was so capable and this unit had a very destructive Image of the Child. My director negotiated a compromise. They promised they would integrate Merrylyn into a regular classroom "as much as she could tolerate," and they agreed to retest her after a shorter than usual interval and reconsider her placement at that time.

I advised Susie, Merrylyn's mother, always to hold on tightly to her belief in Merrylyn and to let that strong Image guide her. That November I got a disturbing phone call from Susie. Family members had visited Merrylyn's Special Education classroom on four different days at various times of day, and each one found Merrylyn sitting in front of a TV watching Sponge Bob!

Susie met with the teacher, the Special Education coordinator and other administrators. At this meeting Susie found out that Merrylyn was only in the regular classroom briefly each day. The rest of the time she spent in the Special Education classroom. When Susie questioned the teacher about watching TV, she was told that *this was part of Merrylyn's education!*

---

61. Videatives are short video clips which George Forman has collected in order to help teachers think through teaching situations. Leslie gave him videos from her classes 2003-5.

PART II: THE DOCUMENTATION PROCESS

The documentation process leads us to improve our understandings, knowledge, and intuitions. Topics emerge — teachers document and wonder and provoke — children respond in an exquisite, often non-linear dance with layer upon layer of meaning. It cannot be planned, but it can be planned for through the teacher's disposition to observe, document, provoke, and think through the preparation of the environment to invite the interactions and encounters through which children's ideas emerge, and through the development of a culture of conversation and construction of theory.

—Pam Oken-Wright

At Diana School in Reggio Emilia, behind the adults we see documentation panels and clay sculptures showing the children's growing understanding of tree growth. Photo: SGC, 1992

What is documentation?

Is documentation the report we hang on the wall, or is it a process integral to the work and lives we lead? Can it be three-dimensional? May it include audio or video recordings? Is it something we *do* or something we *make*?

The answer to all these questions is yes.

We collect data, we think about what we've collected, we consider it with our friends and colleagues and we produce something to share with the children, their parents, the school community, and the wider community.

Leslie and I wouldn't have noticed Reggio ideas and thinking had the Reggiani not brilliantly documented and exhibited and published their work so we could view the enormous events of the children's investigations and their beautiful, thoughtful art.

I first saw a little bit of Reggio Emilia early education on a VHS video, *To Make a Portrait of a Lion*, handed to me in 1989 by Dr. Elizabeth (Betty) Jones, my senior colleague at Pacific Oaks College. Along with the video came a single page of notes about the Reggio Emilia program from John Nimmo. Stunned by the excellence of the work of the children in the video, I watched it again and again and, the next evening, invited my best students to watch it with me. The question that came up, as we watched the children make masterful drawings, sculptures and plays about the lion whose statue stands guard in front of the big church in the market square, was *"How old are these children?"* and the answer, which they had heard before they watched the video, was always, astonishingly, "They leave this school around the time they turn six."

The next time I saw Reggio work it was at the Washington, D.C. National Association for the Education of Young Children conference in 1990, where I spent almost all of my conference time at the *One Hundred Languages of Children* exhibition, which introduced the world to Reggio Emilia work and philosophy. I was trying to puzzle out the work these people were doing with children and its amazing outcomes. Leslie was at that conference too, but we didn't know each other yet.

Separately, both of us were informed, delighted and convinced by the documentation panels we encountered at the Hundred Languages exhibit, and later impressed and amazed by what we saw on the walls of classrooms in Reggio Emilia.

sandbars and asides emerged organically along the way. The Reggiani record and save this material, learning from it at least five times:

1. Participating in the direct experience of the event;

2. Deciding which data to record;

3. Reviewing, sorting and ordering the many photos, transcripts and commentaries, and later choosing those that best tell the story combined with the children's words and adult commentary;

4. Viewing, considering and reflecting on the finished documentation panel with children, colleagues and parents and

5. Considering how the work depicted on the panel might stimulate future explorations and investigations.

These five steps might take months. Let's look at their process in slower motion. Because it's recursive, the documentation process always starts over and over again.

The pieces of the display — photos, quotations from the children, introductory paragraphs, titles, and more — are considered with colleagues many times *before* they are glued down.[70] Questions arise from the collaboration and must be addressed on the panel. The intention is to offer a *well-organized and thoughtfully displayed picture of the children's life, work and learning experiences in a complete, positive, and strong narrative.*

The Reggiani often hang a panel beside a shelf next to the finished artwork — the objects we see being made in the photos and language of the panel. My photograph on page 69 shows clay trees on a shelf, and behind them a panel showing the children's drawings and quoting what they said. On my trips to Reggio Emilia, next to a photograph I saw children's portraits of the person in the photo. Next to the old typewriter I saw drawings of typewriters, and even an ambitious attempt at building a typewriter of clay. An audio recording was tucked into an envelope in the display, and an audio player situated nearby, for listening in on the process.

What's on the documentation panel?

> …Anecdotal observations, samples of children's works, photographs that illustrate a process, transcripts of children's

---

70. I've written elsewhere about the importance of editing. See *http://ecrp.uiuc.edu/v1n1/clemens.html*

"Mine's just a LITTLE crowd."

"They're all friends, so they're all going the same way!"

Others didn't:

"…but in a crowd the people aren't all friends or relatives, you know."

And some were mixed:

"This piece of paper is all filled up. It's a crowd…it's just that people don't all walk with their arms open."

"Yeah, they all look sort of like penguins."

When reminded by a re-reading of what they had said about crowds, these children were now able to skillfully critique their work and go on to *describe what they needed to learn* about how to draw a crowd — they identified the drawing problems and the skills they needed to learn: how to draw people in profile and from the back, how to individuate the people in the crowd, how to vary body positions and more.

"We need to make some from the back and some from the side, not all facing forward."

"I don't know how to do them from the back."

"Me, neither."

"We have to learn how to do it."

"…Listen, you don't know how to do the profile because you need a lot of time to learn how to understand that it's a profile, otherwise they look like monsters."

"I want to say an idea: you have to do the profile one time and then again and again until you learn how."

"Yeah, or else somebody says: 'What kind of a crowd is THAT?[75]'"

Finally a plan for work over the next weeks was becoming clear to the teachers, and over time they set the children tasks that would lead them to accomplishing the hard work of drawing crowds and building them in clay.

75. Ibid, Page 145.

A reciprocal pedagogy leads to many possibilities

In this country, sadly, we have no established, historical image of the teacher as storyteller and historian of the classroom. Instead, our attention is usually directed more towards outcomes, results, products to take home and best scores rather than to the *processes* which create them.

Our new Image of the Child helps us liberate ourselves from what Dr. Malaguzzi called "prophetic pedagogy" — a curriculum that determines what the children will learn *without consulting or studying the children*. We need new perspectives which help us examine many possibilities at once. There is never a *single* solution for the infinite variation we experience while working with children. We must respond in context to the flesh-and-blood children who are with us, and to their very particular, specific intentions. That requires of us flexibility, resourcefulness, responsiveness and reciprocity which unconsidered, conventional, or "canned" curriculum and practices don't allow.[76]

The documentation process drives the curriculum

Without a documentation process a classroom may be wonderfully pleasant, and may help children with their social growth; but for emotional and intellectual growth nothing is as productive as a reflective documentation process that makes a regular time and place for teachers to think and plan collaboratively what they offer the children.

Progettazione and programmazione

The Reggiani distinguish between what they call *progettazione*, projecting or spinning off from interest, as described above, and what they call *programmazione* — delivering a program from a pre-planned curriculum package or lesson plan. If you stay with *programmazione* — the curriculum planned in advance by people who haven't even met your children — your program will rarely experience the kind of excitement and power that emerges from a curriculum based on exploring the passions of the people in the room.

We're exploring and advocating for *progettazione*.

---

76. In 2012 the American Federation of Teachers circulated a petition to end the focus on testing and allow teachers, instead, to respond to the needs they perceive in children. Shocking that this would be controversial!

Reggio documentation is a process occurring *inside* the educational experience, and is essentially about (and central to) inner connections among all the members of the educational village, and *within* each individual element as well. The teacher, the child, the parents, the administrator – *all* are served by thoughtfully created and utilized documentation, since it enriches the process they are all engaging in, and thus themselves.

It deepens their understanding of their own behavior, intentions, and motivations by focusing attention on the core educational issue — the real actions and interactions as they have occurred in the classroom — facilitating user-friendly feedback for all to share.

Documentation provides another perspective by being a review. It allows for timely contemplation and analysis of what has happened, and fresh planning for what happens next. It provides a basis for expanding or contracting interactions. It serves as a landmark from which a better navigational path can be charted. It gives missed opportunities another chance. It can shift focus or emphasis from what was planned to actual occurrences. It can include those who didn't share in the original moment and permits their meaningful and active participation. It supports those formerly passive in becoming active and reactive, thus furthering and enriching their experience.

Properly understood, supported, and utilized, documentation delivers an additional new and unique perspective, the effects of which profoundly change the way we go forward. When we share perspectives and experiences through the documentation materials we generate and create new opportunities and increase the chances that we will go forward differently!

Leslie wrote:, and it's worth repeating: At its best, documentation and the everyday work of the teacher and children become so intertwined that one doesn't exist without the other — each breathes life into the other — the two become one. Their energy is transmitted into the environment, the materials, and into the work of the learning community. If done well, documentation enters and changes the lives of the children, the families, and the understanding of the teacher. If done well, documentation enters and changes the lives of the children, the families, and the understanding of the teacher. This work vitally impacts the hearts and lives of the children, the families and the teacher, provoking further growth for all!

Integration and agency

Documentation is deeply coordinated and incorporated into all parts of the work in Reggio. The Reggiani depend on the documentation process to ensure honest, accurate and comprehensive feedback — to help them research

Why bother to document?

Documenting the children's work is time-consuming, challenging, detailed and finicky. Why do the Reggiani take significant time from their other work to do it? *Because the documentation process grows the whole community.* It grows the teachers who make it, as they reflect on the work of their children, individually and collectively. It grows the children by making their lives visible, fixing and holding these events in their memories.

Documentation also grows the parents, answering their perennial question: What did you learn in school today? It helps the administrator and the world understand this constructivist[79] way of working, which moves beyond worksheets, tests and other academic rituals that purport to "certify" that learning is going on.

Beside the data displayed, Reggio Emilia panels answer questions like these: Where did this panel's story come from? What does it tell us about priorities in this classroom? What does it tell us about how the children are experiencing their time in the learning community? What does it tell parents about their children's lives during the time they are apart?

Looking at data, teachers consider: What's the engagement level of children in the photo? Do they care about this activity as much as we had predicted? More? Differently? The language the Reggiani collect from the children about what's in their photos and their work can tell us how the children conceptualize it — is it different from what the adults expected? Is the *difference* important in telling the story? Many interesting discoveries make their way into panels.

Children's theories

Early in the Shadow project the children are asked to draw "me and my shadow". These baseline drawings show the adults the children's initial understandings and misunderstandings. Later, after weeks of experiences with shadows, the children have learned to predict correctly where a shadow will fall, they can draw complex shadows with multiple light sources, and they have had at least one remarkable experience with making and testing theory.[80]

---

79. The reader unfamiliar with constructivism is encouraged to read Jean Piaget and Lev Vygotsky, both of them important influences on Reggio Emilia thinking.

80. This story was told in the book, Everything Has a Shadow Except Ants published by Reggio Children. *http://zerosei.comune.re.it/inter/reggiochildren.htm* I read this book before I got to Italy. and was interested to see, when I visited Italy, that the children could make other correct predictions not recorded in the book .

- Self-portraits are very revealing, and often the portraits are focused on one body part: eyes drawn very large, with things they see drawn inside (things at the beach, or toys one hopes to have, or what is at the zoo, or the sun, the moon, and the stars).

- Hands are drawn at rest and in conversation, in anger and in joy. Brains are drawn in various forms: thinking and not thinking, angry and happy and trying to be understood.

- Often the Italians will project a large image on a wall, for the children to play "inside" it. An ocean, a sky, a crowd, a square with stone lions in it or whatever is under consideration. The children play inside the scene and it becomes more real to them, readying them to go on to represent it in their individual ways and in their choices of medium.

The wisdom to provide experiences like this comes from collaborative reflection, thinking about data as part of the documentation process. Had the teachers not *paid close attention* to the child's original theory, had they not *collaborated* to figure out how to help the children re-construct their theory, had they not *spent a long time* on shadows, had they tried to give correct information, — risking, and therefore ending the conversation as I did with Hamid who thought the sun was broken[81] — this wonderful piece of intellectual development would have been lost.

When I read through documentation from Reggio I highlight the teacher's language and look very closely at what was said. I ask, how did this adult intervention affect the dialogue? Did it open up the child to more questions? Did it help the children return to the topic? Was it helping children invent theories? ❧

Documentation changes your attitude and understanding

Nicole Mitchell researched changes in college students' attitudes toward documentation before and after they visited Pistoia, an Italian city near Reggio Emilia, very similar in its early childhood programs to those of Reggio Emilia.[82] She reports that one of her students said, "[American] caregivers are unable to use this form of documentation as a curriculum guide because of the focus on kindergarten readiness skills and other restrictions". Another student reported, "[documentation in Pistoia] opened my eyes to the different

---

81. See *page 13*
82. Mitchell, N., *University Students' Perceptions of Pedagogical Documentation: A Qualitative Research Study*. M.A. Thesis, East Carolina University, August, 2010.

CHAPTER 10
Stories about starting to document

A starting place

The idea of making documentation panels may seem overwhelming to you, but documenting develops in stages, not all at once. Remember, the Reggiani have been working with that idea since 1945 (and since 1968 with government support) so they have a head start. With collaboration and practice — and perhaps first beginning with what we call Daily Sheets — documentation displays will come within your reach and be enormously valuable to your whole community. This chapter will show you some early documentation work by people in the United States.

Documentation starts with collecting data

Everyone who thinks in depth about documentation has an individual opinion about *when* it becomes documentation. Yet we can all agree *that what's first collected is data*: the pictures, videos, audio recordings, the notes we take when we have a moment to observe something we see or hear in the classroom, the questions parents ask, the questions children ask, the questions we ask ourselves…all this *undigested* material is data.

Data — photos and audio recordings — are immediately useful, starting as soon as they're taken, to help the children remember, reflect and build on what they've done. In Richmond, Virginia, veteran documenter Pam Oken-Wright hangs new photos with magnets in a place where children can consult them and be reminded of what they were doing. Marie Catrett (see chapter 13) keeps a hard copy of every Daily Sheet on the children's bookshelf in a binder the children called the "Words Letter Book" since the e-mail that comes to their homes is called the "Words Letter".

CHAPTER 11
Thinking about how to document
By Leslie Gleim

Listening

Since our teacher training emphasized our talking, directing, planning — we tend to talk more than we listen. Listening and listening closely is very difficult. When we shift our thinking to the Image of the Child that we've learned from Reggio, and we want to *follow the children's lead*, we must learn to practice *listening*.

Who's getting the practice?

Amelia Gambetti told us in a workshop that early in her teaching she was being supervised by Loris Malaguzzi. Together, they were poring over her documentation of a dialogue in her class. The data showed Amelia asking a question, one child responded, and then she would ask another question, and maybe two children would respond, and then she would ask another question. *Amelia was speaking far more than the children were. She* was getting the practice in language. As they looked at the transcript they could see how many times she spoke and how few times children responded before she spoke again. Her lesson to us was: It is the children who need the practice in speaking, in formulating their thinking into speech, in participating in a conversation. *Not the teacher, who needs practice in listening.*

Observation and documentation help children understand each other

On the Reggio online discussion group a teacher wrote a long description of a child, ending with:

about how children understand gender, parenthood, and other indicators of status.

Notice who the child seeks out. See if he plays with one set of children in the block area but chooses other children when dressing up. Children who are good observers are skilled at choosing productive playmates.

When children play at being cartoon characters or action figures such as Ninja Turtles™ or Power Rangers™, this play rarely develops a complex story line. The children tend to copy what they've seen on television. The longer you watch, the more the children reveal of their frequently extensive, detailed knowledge of the story they've seen on TV. For example, one child playing the blue Power Ranger™ drew out a pretend sword to protect another Power Ranger™ and a third child said, "You can't do that. Only the *red* Power Ranger™ does that." Another four-year-old, this one in family childcare, was so enchanted with Pirates of the Caribbean™ that he would dress up (including eye shadow) and *be* Jack Sparrow.

Observing this kind of repetitious play, teachers often want to see more of the children's creativity and less replaying the TV show. Our task is to offer or promote experiences that are as appealing as the TV events, yet encourage creative expression.[71] The clues to what this expression will consist of are in the details of the behavior you observe:

- What does the Ranger do that's exciting the child?

- Are there dance moves that might give the same satisfaction?

- How does the pirate behave?

- What kind of power is stirring these young children?

Helping children see and hear each other

Teachers can help children to recognize and be respectful of other children's preferences. For example, you can help Roberto notice which children like which foods. As he helps hand out snacks, teach Roberto to ask, "Do you want milk?" When Pete answers "no" you can coach Roberto: "Ask him if he'd rather have water or juice." Tomorrow Roberto can tell the new snack helper Pete's preferences.

---

71. Wassermann, S., Growing teachers: Is there life after Pac-Man? *Childhood Education,* Vol 61(5), May-Jun 1985.

CHAPTER 12
Daily Sheets
By Leslie Gleim

Editor's note: Leslie's Ohio Daily Sheets closely matched the needs of the community where she taught. Leslie sent a copy of her Daily Sheet to each family every day. They really were *daily*, and when one didn't arrive home some parents would phone her to ask where it was. Leslie took their concerns seriously, asking their pardon and explaining what she had been doing instead. She developed Daily Sheets to welcome parents into the process of the classroom. Children, parents and staff all grew through their connections with them. On the next page, you'll see and example of Leslie's Ohio Daily Sheets which were handed to parents at the end of the school day or sent home with the children on the school bus. SGC

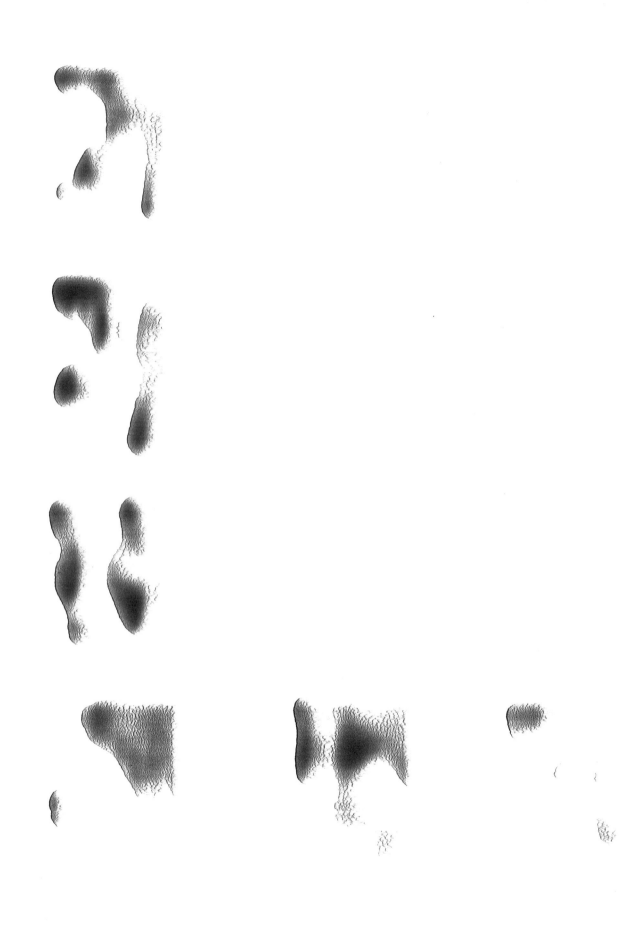

What questions do I ask myself when creating a Daily Sheet?

- What was the central idea or focus for the children today? How do I make it known to the family?

- How does today's work connect to child development theory? Do I have photos of the children doing this work? Have I captured some pertinent children's language or dialogue?

- Does my customary format work with today's material, or does this new material call for another kind of presentation?

- How might I provoke the children to deepen or further their exploration? Can parents help too?

Jargon turns people off, but images and stories draw them in, so I always eliminate technical terms, abbreviations, initials or acronyms by spelling everything out. Similarly, by eliminating some background, I can better focus on what a child is doing, so I crop out anything in the photos that obscures, and highlight what I believe to be important.

When I'm nearly done, I reread my draft of the Daily Sheet. I ask myself if all the parts support a strong Image of the Child and ask myself how today's Daily Sheet fits the flow of our work — how it builds on or emerges from what came before, and what possibilities it suggests for use tomorrow and into the future.

In writing the narrative I often refer to a chart of ages and stages taken from a child development textbook to use as a reference. I don't use their wording but rather explain it using my own words and interpretation.

Example: In the development chart it says "children at age three are able to make + or - marks."

I wrote: Today Kyle, Tyler, Audrey and Tim quickly settled in with paper and markers. After a short while, I noticed them intentionally experimenting. As they paid attention to each other's work, I watched their random scribbles shift to horizontal lines. Audrey began making crosses of her horizontals. The boys, observing her work, began creating their own crosses. How exciting to watch as this group of children extend their thinking and work, connecting early literacy and the child's symbolic thoughts.

on T-shirts. This was my first key into Ryan's world, and I used it to connect with him. Here is my journal of Ryan's experiences with media and some of the questions I asked myself:

9/20 Ryan works in clay. Makes imprints and pokes and scrapes with sticks. When finished he goes to look at a picture book with large images and large letters. Why?

In October and November I made frequent notes about Ryan's intense work in clay. Here are some of the details I saw:

He uses a variety of tools to make marks and to print shapes in the clay. Stays engaged as long as 45 minutes. How can we use his clay work to help him dialogue with his peers or adults? How can we help him connect language with his clay work? Has he made a connection between these marks in clay and the writing he likes on t-shirts?

1/22 Ryan has shifted from poking in the clay to creating lines. Last week I had him feel the smooth clay and then, with my hand over his I made the line and then he would explore it. Once he felt the groove Ryan traced it with his fingers, and then took my hand and moved it as if he wanted more lines from me.

2/2 His scribbling seems purposeful and planned. I'll provide him with chalk, paint, markers, pens, pencils and a variety of papers.

3/9 Ryan explores lines and V shapes. He makes some V's on his paper. I help him work on signing his name. He brings a magnetic letter N to the work table. We worked together. He would make a simple mark and then I would make the same mark. Now it was my turn to change the mark, and he would follow my lead. This game went for 70 minutes once, using up 48 sheets of paper. What connections were made? How can we take this further? Try light table and letters, chalkboard, raised letters, Magna Doodle™.

3/13 Ryan works 25 minutes with clay.

3/21 Now he matches corresponding plastic letters on the light table. Then makes a connection with letters of his name and writes his name!

4/19 Today he made a series of four yellow pictures with crossing lines.

if we worked it right, during nap time we could reflect together on the data we had collected, and also had time to prepare Daily Sheets for parents. Since children didn't attend our school on Fridays we allocated two hours for compiling, processing and planning documentation. Full-time centers have real difficulty finding time to document — but some find ways.

One director I know, committed to the Reggio approach to documentation, meets once a month with her staff after the center closes. They order pizzas or other delivered food and eat from 6:00 to 6:30, and then work together until 8:00 PM. Because the director feels strongly that this type of collaboration and reflection fosters important growth the teachers are paid for their time.

... and in Reggio Emilia

Meeting time is built into the teachers' union contract in Reggio. It is standard practice in Reggio Emilia to review the data, discuss the children, and plan the next stages of the project. Ample time is available for considering what a single bit of data might mean, as well as the meaning of all the data taken together. With time to meet and discuss there's no *rush* to complete a display. ✺

PHOTO TIPS

- The background isn't needed unless it is part of the story, so zoom in!
- Remember when you photograph the children's work to show multiple views: front, back, side, close up of the hands at work, the child's facial expressions showing engagement, wonder, question and surprise.
- Take pictures in natural light whenever you can, with your back to the light source.
- With a digital camera you can take lots of pictures and select only the best ones.
- You can crop easily.
- Always have extra batteries at hand, and keep the camera charged and ready!

All this helps to show the joy of the children's work to others.

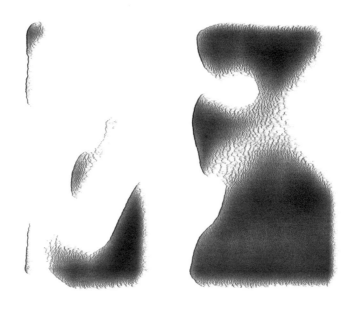

It took Marie a few weeks to collect enough data so she could understand that Elias was fascinated with *trains* — to realize that the various materials he would glide through the air were all imagined to be trains.

The data have led Marie to an important discovery.

After two weeks she shows him a block, asking, "What does this remind you of?" Elias responds, "It's a train!"

After talking about this with me, Marie planned a trip to the train station for her group and their parents. The week before the trip, Marie and the children made a list of things they thought they might see when they got there. The children dictated and Marie printed what they said on a list.

> What do you think we will see at
> the train station?
>
> Nayeli says there will be trains.
>
> Elias says, "I will see an Amtrack train."
>
> Willa thinks she will see toys.
>
> Emerson says he will see a locamotive.
>
> Nayeli thinks there will be windows and a picture
> of a train.
>
> Nayeli thinks all the people at train station
> will need to bring a suitcase.
>
> Elias thinks the Amtrak train will have
> windows.
>
> Nayeli thinks the suitcases will have a
> bar to push it anywhere all the way to
> the bathroom.

Nayeli: What did Emerson say he think he will see?

Marie: (Reading) Emerson says he will see a locomotive.

Nayeli: Okay. (Writing) Emerson says he will see a locomotive. Anything else he said? Okay anything that I said again?

Marie: Here's what I have: Nayeli thinks all the people at the train station will need to bring a suitcase.

Nayeli: Yeah, because you will need to pack up your things in it! And there's a bar to push it where you want to go. If you push it all the way to the bathroom that will be really far!

Marie: Should we write that?

Nayeli: Yeah! (We both write on our lists.)

Marie: Are you finished? May I put your list next to mine?

Nayeli: I forgot to say conductor on it! Conductor, conductor! Little one, little one, (Writes again, a short line). Con-duc-tor. I write about conductor here.

Con-duc-tor. I will give this list to the conductor so that way the conductor will remember that his name was on it.

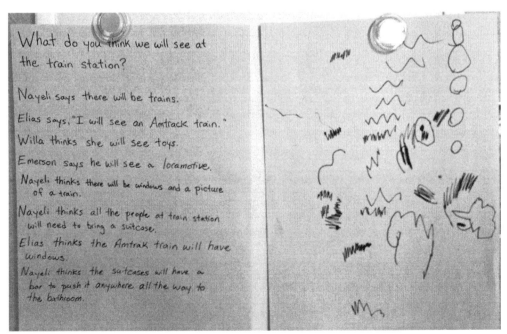

Nayeli: "Now they are both here."

Nayeli finds a passenger with a big suitcase with a bar

Nayeli and Willa document their trip

Elias absorbs the sights and sounds of the train station

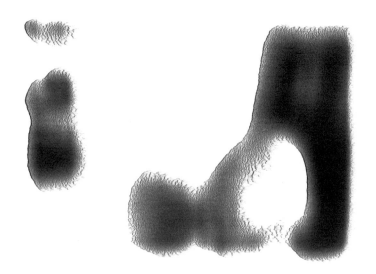

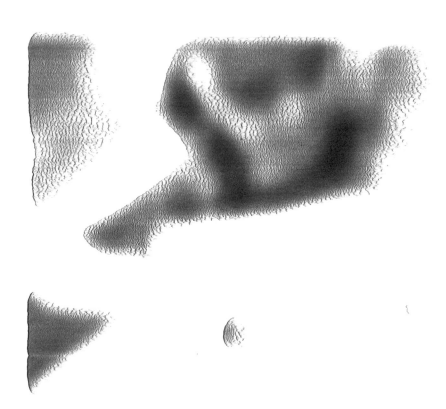

Marie: What did you see at the train station?

Willa: I saw Nayeli. I'll write that on my list.

Marie tells me that Willa wrote several different lists.

Wyatt designs curriculum

Weeks later, Marie *heard* Wyatt tell her that she didn't have enough laundry baskets (she had two at the time — one for laundry, and one to hold drawing paper.) She got four more baskets and the spontaneous play that resulted — underwater, animals in cages, and, lining them up, train play — was wonderful. Her initial intention was to honor Wyatt's idea, but she was amazed (she told me so, repeatedly) when she had no further tasks to do to make this material useful to the children. They knew what to do, and did it! And, of course, they incorporated train play into their basket play!

Train play and basket play merge

Your relationship with the children benefits when you admit your own oversights and shortcomings — like Marie, correcting her undersupply of laundry baskets as a result of Wyatt's complaint — and they see you learning from their ideas or your own mistakes. They observe that this isn't shameful, but rather leads to growth – many children and adults need and appreciate this.

As I was editing this chapter more things happened with the train project — the story isn't over. There is such knowledge and understanding of their

CHAPTER 14
Using a documentation process to identify goals for an individual child and to develop group projects

Children carry out the search for meaning with tenacity and effort, sometimes making mistakes, but they do the searching on their own. We cannot live without meaning; that would preclude any sense of identity, any hope, any future. Children know this and initiate the search right from the beginning of their lives. They know it as young members of the human species, as individuals, as people. The search for the meaning of life and of the self in life is born with the child and is desired by the child. This is why we talk about a child who is competent and strong — a child who has the right to hope and the right to be valued, not a predefined child seen as fragile needy, and incapable.[68]

— *Carla Rinaldi*

Listen, become quiet, watch and wait

Believing that the child is competent, we have to figure out his or her behavior when it seems odd to us. We have to learn to see better. Regularly writing down what we see — *and regularly taking photos and recording* — are tools for improving understanding. To record children's behavior accurately, we first have to quiet ourselves and learn to *see and hear* it. When we have set aside our agendas and preconceptions, we will find out what's going on, and then we can set a course that will support this child.

Editor's note: The rest of this chapter is by Leslie. She presents some stories from the classroom, observing and documenting and acting on her findings. Of course there's no prescription here, you'll have to find your own way. But

---

68. Rinaldi, C. (2001)

Learning from data

I've learned a lot from the data about Lauren that you've sent. These are the troubling behaviors:

- Cutting her own hair
- Poking a child in the face with scissors
- Spitting at children and teachers
- Screaming
- Hitting and kicking teachers and children
- Being easily and frequently distracted from tasks by noise, movement and touch and needing the full attention of one teacher to get through a transition
- Avoiding fine motor tasks, or getting very frustrated while attempting them

Strategies you employ to help her

Here are the strategies you are currently employing to help her:

- Offering a wide range of relaxing sensory activities: waterplay, sand, rocking, etc.
- Warning her verbally before classroom transitions
- Assigning her tasks during those transitions: e.g. she closes the door after everyone's out of the room
- Providing her opportunities to paint and work in clay and other creative activities

These strategies are great — continue them! Lauren may need both words and touch, so placing your hand firmly on her shoulder as you announce a transition may help center her and allow her to attend to what you say. You can also hold her hand during transitions. Perhaps she can even be the person who *announces* a transition from time to time.

First: work on changing Lauren's self-image

Lauren knows how to get people to pay attention to her. When she is violent, people notice her. She makes them mad, and they yell or fuss or punish her. This is who *she has been* in the classroom. You will want to help Lauren see the contradictions between her *behavior* and her *goal* of wanting children to be her friends. Look closely at each of the behaviors on the list. What is the result for Lauren after each of these events? She has learned how to get some

what Lauren does that makes us mad to the *many positive and appropriate things she does*. Over the coming weeks, as you continue to talk with her about this, your job becomes to help her *act thoughtfully* in situations where, customarily, she has simply *reacted*.

Be sure to document Lauren's competence

Start by noticing and writing down moments when Lauren is being competent, purposeful, and non-violent. She will quickly recognize that when she is doing important, constructive, and valuable things you often come by and document them. Not only is she getting attention but now *she has evidence of herself* being competent, to look at, share and enjoy.

Your words, your presence, and your documentation are all positive responses. While you collect data you send a clear and powerful message to Lauren that she is interesting, likeable, strong and capable, *showing her that she is good*. There is a difference. Sydney tells me that she often told children, "You can do hard things! Remember when you did such and such?" When we show children the possibility of living well with others, they learn that social skills are within their reach. And then they reach!

Second: heighten your sensitivity and awareness

As you focus on Lauren, look closely for signals that she's feeling upset, frustrated or anxious — feelings likely to lead to an outburst. Those signals are precursors of loss of control, warnings that she is in trouble, alerting you to redirect and channel her energies into appropriate activities before she resorts to inappropriate actions.

Observe and observe her again, until she shows up in your dreams. When you can figure out what happens *just before* she explodes, you'll have the key. You'll still have to watch closely, in order to intervene before it's too late.[69] Does she become extra restless going from activity to activity? Do you see her begin rubbing her nose indicating frustration, or does she flap or wring her hands? I once worked with a child who started to sweat a moment or two before he would lose control. These signals tell you what this child is feeling inside, feelings that she can't yet put in words. Discovering these signals means you're halfway home. When you detect her signal, go to Lauren and offer her a few appropriate choices: a task, sitting on your lap, work with clay or other calming materials; really anything she loves to do. You know what she loves because you document what goes on in your program. You

---

69. See *One Ball at a Time, page 17*

For example, my classroom assistant couldn't tolerate a child who spit, so if she was tussling with such a child I would relieve her. There are also days when one of us has low energy, and we lean more heavily on the other. Remember and beware — upset children will find and target our vulnerabilities. While you are observing and studying Lauren she is watching and studying you!

Fifth: putting Lauren's strengths to work

Let's use what you told us to try to understand Lauren.

Lauren craves friendship and seeks out the company of children.

A child who wants to be friends with other children has a great incentive. Let's say you have a gentle child who is in need of help with something Lauren is good at. Tell Lauren, "I have seen you build great towers and Molly really needs some help. Could you and Molly work on making a really big tower *together?*" Lauren may say no, and if she does, you can find Molly another helper. But Lauren will probably be glad to show this little girl how to make a great tower. Now you're tapping into her strength and channeling it. There are many possibilities for Lauren to do what she's good at and help other children in the process.

Lauren likes to be a leader and can often be found reading to a group of children or telling a child how they might handle a certain situation.

You can use Lauren's eagerness to help to build your community. As you document her — reading to other children and counseling them — you are showing her the very best of herself! And, as the other children view the documentation photos, they see themselves getting along with her!

Lauren is extremely articulate and when she's calm she's able to retell home stories and reflect on situations.

Another great asset! The key here is "when calm." Use sensory materials with her all day long to help her stay calm. That's no problem because, as you report, she enjoys exploring sensory materials such as goop[71], play dough, clay, water, and paint — anything hands-on and messy!

When she is at loose ends you might suggest: "Lauren, I see you're having trouble deciding what you want to do. Would you like to play with sand or with water or to sit in my lap?" Asking her to choose sends her inward *to see what she wants and feels*, and doesn't allow her to react automatically and

---

71. Goop is a mixture of cornstarch and water. It also has other names: among them *pud, goo,* and *ooblick*

CHAPTER 15
Documenting and projects (go together like a horse and carriage!)

You will usually get your ideas about group projects from either watching or listening to the children as they play and work together and make choices, or studying and analyzing the data you've collected in your documentation process.

The key to a good project is to uncover the children's particular, specific interests and intentions. That often takes a bit of digging. Before initiating a project a teacher will need to observe and document and collaborate extensively. We suggest you begin by documenting for at least a couple of months before you try to launch a project, to become more sensitive and adept at uncovering the children's intentions. The Reggiani usually do a project with a group of 5-8 children, not their whole class. Do what you can to keep groups small.

While the Reggiani usually do a project with a small group of children, you have a different situation, but it is advisable to keep the children in your project group those who have a real interest in the work. Projects begin when the adult recognizes the possibilities. Not everything that the children are interested in can or should become a project. You will have to choose, as Marie did when she built on Elias' interest in trains.[72]

After you've studied the data you collected and a project emerges, you'll continue to collect data during each stage of the project; using it to inform the next day's work and beyond, and saving the data so you can eventually make a panel depicting the project's journey for yourselves and for others, for tomorrow and for ongoing reflection and reference.

---

72. There are good examples of U.S. attempts at this in: *We are all Explorers: Learning and Teaching with Reggio Principles in Urban Settings.* Daniel R. Scheinfeld, Karen M. Haigh, Sandra J.P. Scheinfeld, 2008, Teachers College Press.

Pick up on the children's interests

Several children are showing some interest in boats. What should you do next with this interest? With an audio or video recorder ready, you can ask the children who've been most active in talking about boats and doing things with them to tell you what they're thinking about boats, what they're wondering about — their ideas, their imaginings and their questions. Others can join in the discussion if they like.

"Sam, the other day you were talking about going for a ferry boat ride. Will you tell us about it?" Then just listen, or probe: "What else happened?" "Was there anything scary?" "Were there lots of birds?" "Can you say more about that?" When Sam seems finished, go on with the next child: "Susan, would you tell us how you made your boat?" And, "Peter, let's look at the boat picture you made. What's going on here?" To search further for the children's intention you might put some toy boats near a water table and record and listen to what the children say spontaneously. Hearing the children talk freely will correct, support and extend your understanding of their intention.

Next, looking for the heat of the subject, listen to the tape, and transcribe any sections that seem meaningful to you — the intention of this child, of that child, of the other — what do boats signify to them? Collaborate with adults you respect to find the reasons why each child cares about this subject.

Stages

To summarize the stages of a project:

1. Collect data that shows what's happening in the classroom
2. Locate and frequently refine a topic, collaborating with other adults and aiming to make it align closely with the children's intention. Think of many possible directions the work may take.
3. Pay close attention to what the children discover and supply resources they need to continue. This stage repeats as many times as needed.
4. Allow each project all the time it needs: days, weeks, even months.
5. End with a celebration!

Each of these stages must be collaborative, so the *best intelligence of the community* can be expressed in the work.

If you keep recording, and collaborating with others to analyze what you've recorded, you'll be engaged in progettazione so your projects will be rich and wonderful, and the whole community will celebrate!

CHAPTER 16
Aligning: learning to see from the child's point of view

A wonderful part of thinking about teaching is learning to see a situation from a child's perspective. I call this task "aligning." This can be uncomfortable for grownups — as you rearrange your perspective to be more like a child's you must get closer to the ground psychologically and sometimes physically, and see from what may be an awkward angle — but this child's-eye perspective brings rich results. In *Pay Attention to the Children*[73] I called alignment "reading children's behavior" and told this story:

> As I consulted at a rural childcare program, the teachers pressed me to define carefully what I meant by "reading children's behavior". Since my first explanations didn't seem to help, I promised that when it happened I'd alert them. Later that day they had the children outdoors in the summer sun, most of the children in a wading pool and two others at an easel, and Steve ran from the wading pool over to the easel, swiped his finger across the paint, and then painted on his body. The caregivers cried out to him that he wasn't to do this, that he was spoiling Terry's painting, and that he must stop. A few minutes later, when the adults no longer were paying attention to him, he cheerfully repeated the whole scene. The teachers repeated their outcry, this time in a slightly angrier tone.

> I asked if I could step in, and show them how I was *reading his behavior*. With their permission I asked him, "Steve, if I give you some paint for body-painting, will you leave Terry's

---

73 *Pay Attention To the Children, Lessons for Teachers and Parents from Sylvia Ashton-Warner,* Available from my website: *www.eceteacher.org*

the same, uniquely human, perspective — wanting to know, to accomplish, to grow, to follow their imaginations and curiosities. The teacher, caring, adds her own desire to help the child achieve his own intention.

Nel Noddings[74] writes that caring is not something you are, but is something you engage in, something possible in every interaction. In every connection with another we have the potential opportunity to enter into a caring — or uncaring — relation. In her view, each caring encounter is an interaction between a person giving care and a person or object receiving care; a "one-caring" and another or an object, "cared-for." The "one-caring" responds to the "cared-for" with full attention and receptivity to who or what the "cared-for" is and needs. This closely describes the exchange of energy in the Reggio Image of the Child:

> The caring teacher strives first to establish and maintain caring relations, and these relations exhibit an integrity that provides a foundation for everything teacher and student do together.

Noddings' concept goes beyond empathy and describes a state of *seeing and feeling with* the other. The carer must be attentive to what the cared-for is feeling and trying to express. This calls for alignment.

Noddings writes:

> When I care, my motive energy begins to flow toward the needs and wants of the cared-for. This does not mean that I will always approve of what the other wants, nor does it mean that I will never try to lead him or her to a better set of values, but *I must take into account the feelings and desires that are actually there and respond as positively as my values and capacities allow.* [My emphasis]

The disposition to alignment

As we try to change our Image of the Child from *one who is weak and needs us to protect him* to *one who is strong, competent, and has his own ideas, needing us to find the materials and times for him to explore and create*, we are called on to make changes in our own teaching dispositions.[75] Most of us haven't had a mentor who was focused on helping us learn to supply a group of children with materials and experiences that help them explore what they care about.

74. Noddings, N. (2005) 'Caring in Education', *The Encyclopedia of Informal Education,www.infed.org/biblio/noddings_caring_in_education.htm*
75. Katz, Lilian G. ERIC Clearinghouse on Elementary and Early Childhood Education, Urbana, IL. *Dispositions as Educational Goals.* *http://eric.ed.gov/?id=ED363454*

Often, when I visit programs for young children, the adults, seeing me as an authority figure, immediately turn to the nearest child, pointing to something and asking "What color is this?" — as if that is what I came to hear them say. These adults believe their job is testing the children for factual knowledge.[77]

They are genuinely surprised when I tell them that I believe the curriculum *shouldn't be* about knowing your colors, but about *knowing how to learn* — wanting to know how to learn, engaging with something you find important. We have an obligation to encourage the terrific thirst *to make sense of the world* little children experience from the day they are born.

When we work and align with children, we see how very alert they are to information (and the style of its delivery) and how very eager they are to learn the things that interest them. The two-year-old at the beach in the sand with just a pail and a shovel is content. Her attention span is not short. She'll let you join her play, or you can leave her alone, as long as she has access to the beloved sand, the water, and the tools. The four-year-old playing fantasy games with Barbies™ or other dolls, or with toy cars, trains, blocks or dress-up clothing usually doesn't get into trouble as long as there is space and time for the things he or she wants to do. In Chapter 13[78] we saw the possibilities of laundry baskets, a curriculum designed by a four-year-old. Trouble comes when the space is too small, the supplies are scarce, or time is limited — and the curriculum doesn't align with their interests or their needs.

Pacing

Leslie writes:
The Italians remind us: "I bambini e le bambine hanno bisogno di tempo." (Little boys and little girls need time.)

Observing an adult and child walking together we usually see one of three scenarios: the child hurries, pulled by the adult who is focused on getting to a destination. Or, the adult chafes as the child explores the grass in the cracks of the sidewalk. Or, the adult slows down and marvels as the child examines every crack in the cement, every bug, every passer-by — enjoying the long time "little boys and little girls need."

When that small person beside you reaches up and takes your hand and you walk side-by-side what speed do you go? Who paces that walk? The realization, at the moment you recognize how much you must slow your adult

---

77. See Baby Talk *page 203*
78. See *page 121*

You were less than whole?
How could anyone fail to notice
That your loving is a miracle,
How deeply you're connected to my soul.

If you record yourself teaching you can hear when you're being judgmental, and when you're leaving children the space to be themselves. Practice so you can easily and respectfully share power with the children. Sooner or later you'll hear yourself trying to *get* what the child's saying. This is a skill you can cultivate, and as you become skillful, children will learn more, and more comfortably, from you!

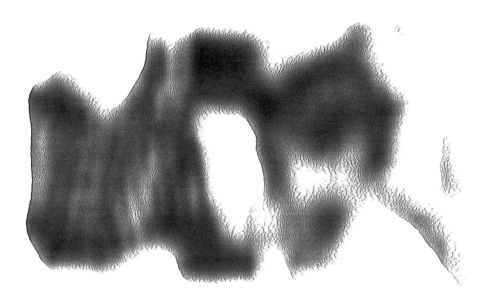

and information, as humans have always done, to create theories about mysterious phenomena such as the source of rain.

Learning to consider alternatives and test hypotheses is more important than knowing answers! Answers can be located using search engines, but clear thinking must be constructed by each of us. So we don't rush to answer a child's question. Instead we inquire, "What's going on here?" or "What story is this?" or "What can you tell me about this?" or "How can we find out if the sun's broken?" and let the child explore his question more fully.

When we problematize, we make the problem the focal point of thought, bring intelligence to the problem, and break it down into components. We let the *problem* be what we're thinking about, rather than rushing ahead to a solution. Here's an example from Reggio:[81]

The Crowd Project

Many of the children in a school in Reggio had been to the seashore during summer vacation and their teachers had provisionally planned a project to explore seashore experience: aquatic life, both animal and vegetable. They had brought out shells, pebbles, and sand for the children to explore. But after the first discussion about summer took place and the teachers listened to the recording they'd made of the discussion, they heard highly charged statements *not* about the ocean and the seashells, but about the *crowds*. So they changed their project plan, and followed the children's excitement and anxiety into a project about crowds. To remind you: the children, in a group of girls and another group of boys, described crowds in detail.

Soon after their discussions, the children were asked to draw a crowd. Their crowds looked like rows of paper dolls lined up across the page, all alike, all facing in the same direction.

Then the adults read the children descriptions of the crowds from the transcripts of recordings of yesterday's discussion. Next they asked the children if their drawings matched what their conversation described. You can see the children's comments on beginning on *page 76*. The teachers were problematizing when they asked the children to compare the crowds they drew with how they described crowds in words.

After the children had determined the things they wanted to learn about crowds, they set to work. Children drew and sculpted portraits of each other from all sides. They studied photos of crowds, and practiced walking like a

---

81. See *The Hundred Languages of Children*, the catalog of the 100 Languages exhibit, second edition.

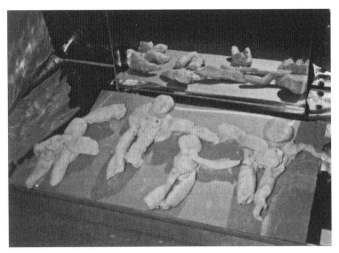

Photo: SGC, 1988

I was distressed by this display. To me the work looked like dead bodies, and I saw the *absence of teaching* here. I wanted the teacher to check in with the child, clearly new to clay work, who made these people: "Your people are lying down. Did you want them to be lying down?" If the child said no, (as I think he would have) the teacher could have said, "There are lots of things you can do with clay, to make bodies be the way you want them to be. Let's work on *making them be the way you want them to be*." The teacher could set aside times for working with any children who might want to explore how to make clay people who look alive.

During their first meeting, the teacher could offer, "I can help you figure out how to make people stand up or sit down, whatever you want. We could look at some pictures of clay people, and see how other artists made them." The children could analyze the pictures, or look at little dolls that can stand and sit, and try again. (The manikins sold at art stores are great to have in early childhood classrooms.)

You can teach children how to join clay pieces — by scoring and then painting with slip (liquid clay). Marie Catrett has found you can give children a wet toothbrush to accomplish the task of scoring and slipping at the same time. Another route to live clay people is to use metal, wood or paper props to help the people be vertical until they harden. Children of this age are absolutely able to make people who aren't dead, but they may need your help to get started.

If you're going to provoke a child to complete her intention, you'll need to articulate your offers and be prepared to help. "Is it finished? Is it the way you want it? Are you satisfied with it?" You want to make clear that *if the child isn't*

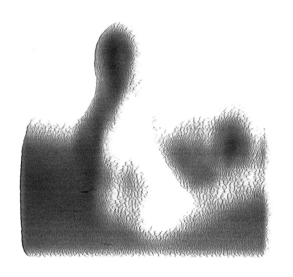

- Feedback ("your people are lying down") can come to be seen as a step on the path to accomplishment (learning to make clay people in postures you like!)

- You can do hard things!

There's no "right way" to do art. Art is the expression of the artist, and children can revise their own work if they want it revised. It's appalling when a teacher "fixes" a child's artwork, to make it "better." A teacher who aligns with a child artist will ask if the child got the result she intended. The teacher can be helpful, not by taking over, but by offering techniques that would bring the child closer to her goal.

A letter to a teacher trying to think in Reggio ways: It's tough going against the traffic

Dear Teacher,

How frustrating that your school doesn't encourage you to restrain yourself from offering factual explanations to children when, for example, they're interested in the rain cycle. Current educational trends lead one to always supply and test children on facts. But Reggio thinking takes for granted that it's more important for the children to *speculate* about what might be the ways the rain cycle operates — to create theories and discuss *their* different ideas, and to draw or otherwise depict them — than it is for them to learn facts from *your* instruction.

If you decide to adopt this approach you'll likely be going against traffic. Parents may be worried: "will they know enough?" or "will they be able to get into good schools?" Educate yourself deeply about this: why you're going upstream, why you believe considering problems and making theories will serve the children better than you giving them isolated facts, what the parents fear and how you are going to help them through those fears so they can advocate well for their children. Before you are able to influence parents you must be prepared, able to articulate and to share your own confidence and theories. You must also be prepared to listen closely to what the parents have to say.

The Reggio way often leaves the children in a state of disequilibrium; perhaps they won't KNOW as many answers as other adults want. You might tell parents: "We've been thinking about and exploring helping children develop some habits of mind that will, in the long run, make them better thinkers. This means we don't always answer their questions, but instead we give children room to experiment with their own ideas. "Will you share with us when

Children in my classroom listening to me read a story, 1973. Photo by Peeter Vilms.

CHAPTER 18
Talking with children

Authentic praise

We visit classrooms and childcare centers and homes and hear teachers, parents and caregivers say, "Good job!" or "Beautiful!" or "That's nice!"

When you align with a child, you don't say "good job". It tells the children that you're the judge and there's a specific *right way* for them to do this task, and if you do it the right way you will get feedback from the judge who says "good job." This carries the message: "You will do things to please others, not learn to find your own individual, satisfying ways to do things." This is the opposite of trying to understand and appreciate the child's own intentions, the opposite of caring, and of listening. These automatic responses don't carry an authentic message.[83] They don't invite a child to think about what she intends for her work. These automatic responses say that the teacher likes what the child did, whatever it is. They don't say *why*, and they are given out to everyone, regardless of whether there's real thought and care in the work, or not. As such they have low value.

---

83. An incredibly valuable resource for learning supportive language is *Choice Words,* by Peter H. Johnston, Portland, ME Stenhouse Publishers, 2004. It has been the subject of great discussions on the Whole Language online discussion group and in our SF Reggio group.

Making theories

Even if our theories about how things work are dead wrong, *making theories* is a great habit of mind. Adults can unpack children's incorrect theories collaboratively, looking for good provocations to help the children review and re-construct their thinking. During the Shadows Project[84], a child developed the elegant, though incorrect, theory that things that move have shadows that move, and things that are stationary have stationary shadows. In response, the teachers took the children to the plaza, where there were columns in front of the Municipal Theater. They traced with chalk the outline of the shadow of one column. The children predicted that the shadow would be in the same place when they came back at lunchtime, but, of course, it wasn't. This made the children reconsider their theory and revise their thinking about shadows and they discovered *they had to consider the position of the sun* in all their shadow drawings.

Good questions

Do ask the questions *What's going on here?* and *What's happening?* This is a great intervention for an adult to make, when stopping to chat with a child at work. Rather than demanding an answer, these questions *invite* a dialogue, opening the opportunity for discussion. If the child has things to say, she'll respond to "What's going on here?" On the other hand, if the child seems to want you to leave her to her work, go away!

I observed Pam Oken-Wright asking children "Are you satisfied?" and have thought about and discussed it with other people since. Pam also asks her children when they think they've finished a piece of art, to take it to other children, asking them if they have suggestions. You can teach children to show finished work to another and ask: "Are there bits to add or change to make it better?" This is a good alternative to "Do you like it?"

When a child brings you a piece of work and says it's finished, if he has some idea of what he wants the piece to be, then you can ask him, *Are you satisfied?* This question gives the child authority, and lets him be the judge of the quality of what he has made. Of course, "are you satisfied?" *must be a genuine inquiry*, not a statement of your judgment, but instead about the child's own judgment. It is not the only response, but one that in the right situation can support a child learning to ask himself for his best work. *If you ask only when you're dissatisfied the children will feel you're controlling them, sensing a judgment rather than a caring, aligned interest.*

---

84.   See *Everything Has a Shadow Except Ants. www.learningmaterialswork.com*

Don't ask, "Can you tell me?" The child will feel inadequate if he can't. Instead of "Can you tell me what happened?" simply ask "What happened?" Instead of "Can you tell me what color the wastebasket is?" simply ask "Get me the brown wastebasket." The children will learn their colors, don't worry!

Asking your colleague

Sometimes we see or hear our colleagues stressing out — losing their calm or perspective or balance. We want to help. Long ago I had a wonderful teaching partner, Ann Brown[86], with whom I made an agreement. If either of us heard something we didn't find comfortable, she would go to the other and say "Do you *mean to be doing* what you're doing?"

We agreed we'd accept the answer, whatever it was. If the reply was *I'm NOT doing what I mean to be doing*, the calm teacher would take over what the other was doing, and let her go wash her face or walk around the block before she returned to teaching. If the reply was "I'm ok," we agreed that the one asking the question should just walk away.

Stop looking for correct answers. Instead, construct better questions!

The elementary schools most of us attended pushed us to focus exclusively on producing correct answers, but we often didn't know why or how we got to them.[87] Many of us don't know *why or how* our cars or computers are able to do what they do. We know when the car runs smoothly, but not how to adjust the carburetor. Similarly, we know there's a food pyramid, but not what constitutes good nutrition. Thinking about this, we want something better for our children.

When we concentrate on getting right answers or results we often lose sight of processes. Try to explain why our way of doing long division gives us correct answers — almost none of us can explain it, even though we can *do* long division. We learned the *algorithm* (what to do first, second, and third, to produce the correct answer) but not *why* it worked.

---

86. After starting The Discovery Room for Children in New York City with me, Ann went on to start and direct The Newark Center for Creative Learning, in Delaware. She was there until her retirement in 2001.
87. Selma Wassermann in *This Teaching Life* suggests that our cultural emphasis on right answers is problematic.

exactly what dictionaries do regularly, as new editions report today's revisions of yesterday's standard usage.

Words are among the many things we re-examine as we learn to see with Reggio vision. How should we choose which words to use with children? Which words, importantly, should we not use? Do we help the children grow up with a vocabulary which looks to an egalitarian future where everyone blossoms? Can our words help bring about a future in which women and men are equally honored and respected? Are we preparing for a future using evenhanded language that ascribes equal dignity to peoples of all continents?

Lazy Susan

In 2008 on the Reggio online discussion group someone used the term *Lazy Susan* and I suggested *turntable* as an alternative. The pejorative *lazy* linked with the female name *Susan* isn't the message we want to pass on to children. I believe that third grade is about the right time for children to become familiar with Standard English, to practice it, and to learn that its use is expected in many arenas, especially the work world. In the long sweet days of early childhood, the important thing about language is to speak as those you love speak, and to understand as many people as you can. A child speaks locally, even as we encourage her to think globally.

As one whose parents learned their English from the radio, because *their* immigrant parents spoke with accents, I speak and write standard English. I also enjoy all the other forms of English I hear — different accents or changes in word order because that's the way it's spoken in someone's home; Black English with its rich images and swift comebacks; country language and neighborhood dialects like Brooklyn and Cockney, and Welsh and Australian and New Zealand English as well. I like them all, and the new generations of meaning and usage that come into play when I'm not looking — for example, that *bad* is the new good!

The only words that offend me are those used to diminish others

Children hear words literally. One boy, after his grandmother's death, participated with the family in every aspect of mourning — until he was invited to "view the body". He shrank in horror, although he had accepted the idea of death very calmly. When a wise relative talked with him, trying to find the source of this horror, he discovered that the child thought "the body" meant it would not include a head.[89]

---

89. This incident is described in *Good Grief, Helping Groups of Children When a Friend Dies*, by Sandra Sutherland Smith, a book we believe teachers of young children should read and keep on hand before it is needed. Sadly, it's out of print; try *www.abebooks.com* for used copies.

This is the kind of sensibility we wish teachers would have about gender issues. We don't need lazy images of girls or women, who are already over-programmed for passivity by much of advertising and television.

Sometimes someone asks if we can be *too* sensitive about this subject, but the more important question is: can we become overly *desensitized*? Do we teachers become passive, just maintaining the status quo? Isn't it better to sift and scrutinize words and the images that the words convey?

Labels and Reggio

Leslie writes:
Since a large part of my experience is with the world of special education and all its vocabulary, I listen to adults and children talking about someone's differences and I want to help them learn that differences can suggest positive, interesting possibilities.

I lived in the heart of Appalachia where stereotypes abound — people are called illiterate, poor, lazy, hillbillies. My advocacy for sensitivity emerges from both of these worlds. I want to emphasize the dignity and ability of people, able-bodied or not, who come from any place.

How does this relate to the Reggio journey? Negatively labeling children who are atypical subverts our Image of the Child. It is in early childhood that our images of the world and the nuances and connotations that are associated with the spoken word come into being. If we are going to change society we must begin with the young children.

Our classroom culture and language should honor all. In Reggio they say, "Io chi siamo" or "I am who we are" meaning that our classrooms should embrace, reflect and respect the many different experiences and points of view of our diversity. Openness and inclusiveness expands the children's horizons, and our own. There can be no harm in reinventing how words are used in the context of our learning community. In our documentation and in communications to parents we need to share with them why we use some words and avoid others. ᏠᎧ

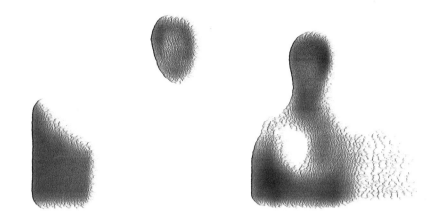

How does a child learn to read *in context*? While planning and recording project work the letter *c* will appear in children's notes about the clay, their interest in candy, or their friend Carla — and this will show them *c* at work, representing its sound. In Reggio Emilia each classroom has a set of pigeon-hole mailboxes, labeled with the children's names. Most days children draw and write messages to each other, an activity which begins in September. They put their drawings and little presents in each others' mailboxes, and this quickly leads the children to be aware that they need letters — including *c* — which adults gladly supply.[90]

On our playground, 1973. Photo by Peeter Vilms.

Valuing the arts for expression and communication

Children do art every day — *every day* — in Reggio. I saw three- and four-year-old children there who were already at the stage of making patterns of letters and numbers. Nobody told them to, but this is what appeared when they were supplied with excellent quality markers, good paper, and relaxed time.

In Reggio, children are educated to be skillful

Children in the Reggio schools work in clay and draw, they paint and build with many materials, they sew and they hammer and they do papier mache.

---

90. I've written at length about Ashton-Warner's Key Vocabulary, the most useful way that I have found to teach beginning reading in English. See my books: *The Sun's Not Broken* and *Pay Attention to the Children.*

Parachute play in my classroom, 1972. Photo by Peeter Vilms

CHAPTER 20
Working together

If you're looking for how the day works in Reggio Emilia, read one or more of these books about projects from Reggio: *Everything Has a Shadow Except Ants*, or *Shoe and Meter*, or *The City*.[91] You'll find discussions about how the curriculum emerges and develops, as well as other clues to their day. If you want a more systematic description of the parts of the day, read Edwards, Gandini and Forman, *The Hundred Languages of Children*.

There's a huge amount of planning in a classroom where adults align with children. Where will the atelierista be today, and with whom? What needs to be purchased, taken out of storage, set up for the work that is planned? What is the data collected yesterday saying about what needs to happen next in the project? At the start of the Reggio day adults talk together briefly about the appointments of the day, and about what will be needed, and they share responsibility for keeping the day moving.

We North Americans can't copy Reggio, but we can use the structures they've developed to figure out what our work should be

The teachers in Reggio Emilia have developed their program to suit *their* children and community. These Italians trust their children will learn whatever they need to learn, when they need to learn it! They don't have *No Child Left Behind* or *Race to the Top* to contend with. And their work is less demanding because they work in Italian — a phonetic language — unlike English which

---

91. You can order these books from *www.learningmaterialswork.com*

come into the classroom *to something they really like.* This makes the transition much easier. Don't follow one teacher-directed activity with another, do alternate active times with quiet ones. Everyone likes to have some variety and some choice.

If you question every minute of the day you'll eliminate the pot roast.[93] Your work will become responsive to the children. That's an enormous change for most people, bringing them joy and sidestepping teacher burnout.

When will the children learn academic facts?

In Reggio, a lot of facts are learned during classroom investigations and projects. We don't want children to think of learning as dry and disconnected — as a way of memorizing what other people want us to know. We don't want children looking at our *faces* to see what answers we expect from them. We want them going inside themselves to learn what they want, identifying their own questions and goals. We want them to become independent, empowered agents — exploring their own ideas and making the differences in the world that they would like to see. Additionally, we want them listening to other people to learn that we are all interesting, we all have different points of view — and that good ideas can come from everybody.

If they love learning because it has come in response to *their wants and needs*, the children will be better able to tolerate inappropriate teaching when they encounter it later. They'll use Google, Dogpile and the library for facts, and they'll begin to understand that *their own thinking* — making, discussing, drawing, comparing and checking out theories — is what's central to an education. They will be prepared to think about group projects when they enter "big schools" — collaborating, representing their ideas in media, and celebrating — all will be part of their understanding of how people work together.

In the meantime, they'll be watching adults collaborate and make sensible changes, and they'll be trying some collaborations of their own. What a good contagion that will be! Remember, niente senza gioia! (Nothing without joy!)

93. See *page 23*

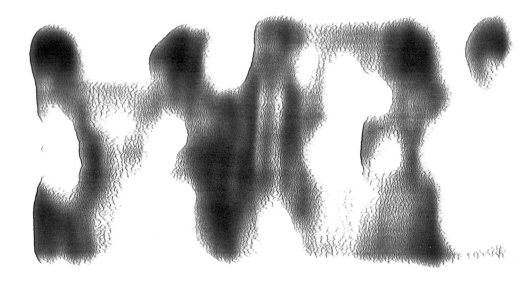

CHAPTER 21
It's not a system: Montessori isn't Malaguzzi

A Montessori-trained teacher told me that she wasn't satisfied with the work she was doing. "I want to learn how to train myself to be a Reggio teacher." I told her that when you finish Montessori training you've learned Montessori, but Reggio *doesn't work that way.* The Reggio Emilia approach demands that you continue to reflect — forever —on what you are seeing and that you continue refining your understandings, learning from your experiences to modify your practices. Reggio work is a process, not a destination. You *become* a Montessori teacher, but you keep *learning from* Reggio ideas.

Reggio thinking and practice plunges you into the process of regularly recreating yourself. You look at what you did and what the children did and what surprised you and *based upon the information in those surprises you choose* what you want to do next. You learn from today what you'll do tomorrow. The point is not "I want to do Reggio," but "I want to become the best teacher I can become, the way teachers do in Reggio. What can I learn from them?"

You become more self-aware as you deepen your relationships with children, parents and colleagues. You learn to do things, see what happens, and reflect alone and collaboratively. You'll never understand anyone else's learning process as well as you can understand your own. Nobody can teach you what you must construct for yourself.

Others can help you raise your awareness: a director or in-service instructor or anyone in charge of developing teachers does well to warn folks: "I will ask you *why you do what you do.* If you don't know, I'll ask you to discontinue it until you have a reason. Better to let the children choose what *they* want to

Remember, we have to find out a child's intention since it isn't always apparent, and we must learn to watch for signals. We try to support a child's intention as soon as we can, and in the best ways we can, but *without taking away the child's initiative or his hands-on experience*. We have to overcome our impulse to say "No, that's too hard for someone as little as you are" and to figure out, instead, what we *can* do to further the child's intention.

Did I learn much about the Reggio Emilia approach in Italy? Sure, and even more from watching Americans (and New Zealanders and Australians and Canadians) struggle with ideas from Reggio and seeing what emerges as they attempt to integrate these ideas into their local practice. I advise someone interested in Reggio to join the Reggio Emilia online discussion group,[94] to begin to document, to follow Leslie's website[95], to share ideas, to read books (see our bibliography), and to talk with other people about these ideas.

Instead of correcting language...

How can you respect the children's work, avoid interrupting the flow of their speech, yet extend their language? You don't need to fix the language at the moment you hear it. Instead, use what you heard and noted, and repeatedly model the language you want the child to learn. I suggest you photograph the child at the activity where you heard the error, and later, looking at the photos together, you discuss the activity. In this way you've frozen the event in time and respected the activity. Language is learned gradually, slowly, over time and through repetition. You can afford to pick your times and places carefully. The documentation process helps you find these times and places, as the children become better known to you. For example: Once you have a note about a language error you might make a game to help that child, either alone or with a couple of other children.

Separating children by gender

When I was in Reggio I saw the adults separate girls from boys to do the same activity. This occurred on several occasions. I wondered at this, coming from my own co-educational, feminist background. I put the question to one of the teachers there: Do you separate the boys and girls in order to make them more different from each other, or more alike? At first, the teacher said she had never been asked this question before. Then she took a moment and responded: "To make them more alike." She gave me the following example:

---

94. There is a link to do this from my website: *http://www.eceteacher.org/links.htm*
95. *www.midpac.edu/elementary/PG*

Stephanie Edgeworth, a highly capable Australian teacher, asked the children what they expected to see on their bus trip. Then she prepared a grid (or Lotto sheet) using their drawings, and gave each child a copy, so they could check off what they saw on the trip.

Reggio Emilia work is about staying conscious of the unique events that occur, and imagining and learning from them what the many possibilities for next steps might be. It cannot be planned, in specifics, but you can prepare mindfully and expect likely events. Or, you can plan in detail if you're *very very good at letting go of what you've planned.*

thought and experience. Sharing our viewpoint and knowledge with parents is an integral part of our task. It can be challenging, but it mustn't be avoided.

I've worked with many African-American parents in poverty with a history of being alienated by their schools, who, after watching me for the first few months, found me to be someone with respect for their culture and their children. *After they trusted me* these parents listened carefully to me. They wanted insights from me, and to explore my analysis of how they could best support their children, just as I wanted their perceptions about their children to inform my own.

On the other hand, I've worked with some privileged parents who wanted me to be their servant, taking their orders and doing only as they saw fit with their children. Often this meant "preparing" children with the kind of decontextualized work I despise, in order to get their children into the "best schools". The traditional curriculum focus of colors, shapes, holidays, and rote calendar recitation about numbers and days of the week doesn't support living joyously or deeply, so I won't follow it. I believe that children are entitled to a joyful life, and to explore their world in depth. I think that living well today is the *very best* preparation for whatever comes next.

It was harder to work with these privileged parents, since I had to be faithful to my own principles yet still listen carefully and thoughtfully to what the parents demanded. Sometimes I was able to show them how my activities satisfied their long-range goals For example, I taught their children to read, rather than teaching them the alphabet. Other times we couldn't find common ground, and they left the program.

These two very different groups of parents suggest that the Reggio focus on context: "It depends" is necessary and correct. There should be a good fit between parent and teacher, and when there isn't, it is necessary to somehow resolve differences. If that's not possible, parents will need to find programs that work for them. (Teachers could concede, of course, but ethics require that we practice what we seriously think is best for children.)

Ideally the children will benefit from *parents and teachers sharing their best thinking*, taking an experimental attitude to bring greater information and understanding where there are differences, and always trying to think in terms of what supports strong healthy feelings and thinking in young children.

CHAPTER 23
Expanding problems so children learn to find solutions: Science and critical thinking

> *I hear...and I forget*
> *I see...and I remember*
> *I do...and I understand*
> — Ancient Chinese Proverb

Most teachers *give young children the answers* to the scientific questions they raise. Children often lose these answers and repeat their questions. By contrast, adults in Reggio Emilia schools *avoid* supplying answers. Instead, they teach children *to work in the way scientists work:* investigating and examining things. They help children make careful observations, and represent those observations by drawing, sculpting or other media — and expressing themselves in the Hundred Languages the children grow to understand in greater depth. I find this arts-as-a-way-into-science approach very appealing and effective. I think it can shift us away from the poor relationship many early childhood teachers have with science, to an intellectually grounded positive realignment. Children come to understand that science is rooted in our real world, the world they can see and represent in their artwork and they also come to see that science is full of practical and useful methods *they* can employ to express, symbolize, and represent their world and themselves.

Problems are opportunities! You can help children construct their knowledge

It is a customary Reggio practice to make a problem out of things often not perceived as problems (problematize them) — and *then* to work on solutions. When we do this, problems become our friends; we get to know them and then we learn good stuff.[96]

---

96. See *page 38* where the teachers problematize the issue of crowds, and this leads them to a multi-part project whose goals were indicated by the children in their discussion about why their initial crowd drawings weren't good enough.

Nowadays I try very hard to inhibit my desires to help children "correct themselves", or to hurry them to a conclusion. This continues to be a big, difficult change to make in myself. These days, I try instead, to admire the passion and discernment in the children's views, and to find the theories their positions seem to indicate.

Pam told me, when I asked later on, that each girl maintained her own initial position about the primacy of heart or head, but after they had discussed it at length, each child was more able to tell why the other side thought as they did.

at a time. This feat amazed their friends. In this lesson, there were elements of *self-esteem, motor control,* and most of all, you *knew you couldn't* stand on your head when you started and you *knew you could* when you finished. This lesson also helped introduce the idea of *learning from a teacher* for children who didn't yet understand it.

Jumping! 1972, Photo: SGC

I've written a great deal, elsewhere, about Key Vocabulary, the method of early reading instruction taught to us by Sylvia Ashton-Warner.[99] When I was teaching young children, my lessons with them — collaboratively finding the words that had power and impact for each child — were wonderful lessons for *me* about *who the children were and what they cared about.* And they were wonderful for the children, helping them name and begin to control important things and relationships in their lives. I tried to see each child for a three- to seven-minute lesson two or three times each week, and these lessons were the backbone of my program. Since reading English is much harder than reading Italian, which is phonetic, we have

99. *The Sun's Not Broken, A Cloud's Just in the Way; On Child-Centered Teaching,* and *Pay Attention to the Children: Lessons for Teachers and Parents from Sylvia Ashton-Warner.* You can order them from me at *www.eceteacher.org* Copies of TSNB will be used ones.

repeat the name and go on. We played this every day until all the children could successfully complete the circle of names. I wanted all the children in our group to really acknowledge each other, and knowing names was necessary. As children accomplished naming their classmates around the circle, we cheered and clapped for each success, and in a two or three weeks, all had succeeded!

This game came from my own failing. Since I often forget names — even ones I really shouldn't forget — I have learned to ask "Would you remind me of your name?" If children forget someone's name, I teach them to use this phrase — or something similar — giving them an enduring, courteous skill to deal with a common problem.

Naming is different in different cultures. Among many African-Americans everyone in one's generation is a "cousin" — whether or not he or she is the daughter or son of an aunt or uncle. Mother and grandma may be "mama" and "big mama". Names are not always used in exactly the way that European-Americans are accustomed to. Working mostly in the African-American communities of Harlem and Bayview-Hunters Point, I learned that other titles are used there and found that I could best respond to this difference by learning what people meant, asking respectfully — "What would you like me to call you?" and accepting and using the reply.

When I taught Mexican-American and other Latino children, I learned not to correct them when they called me "teacher" or "maestra" instead of Sydney, as the other children did. In their culture this is a mark of great respect. In the early days of the school year it didn't feel right to challenge what they wanted to call me. Later in the year I taught them that schools in this country generally expect teachers to be called by name — but this was not to correct them, but rather to provide *another way* to address a teacher, and I taught it only after establishing a relationship we built together, over time.

I did a project with first graders in which they learned where their names came from. They were assigned homework: to interview their grownups to find out the story of their names and then to report what they had found to the class. The stories were wonderful and varied, and, told at the beginning of the year, they helped us to know each other better and to learn to call each other by name.

This work with names was more like units or lessons from my pre-Reggio teaching. Why a lesson instead of exploration? To me, helping the children relate well to each other and build our community made everything that followed happier and easier.

CHAPTER 25
Finding and extending the child's intention

Harnessing *hot cognition*

How do we identify the child's strong curiosity and interest and *where* she is in her thinking, and move her engagement to a deeper level? *How and when* do we scaffold her learning so she can accomplish her intention? How does this work in a group?

I've been interested in "hot cognition" — teaching based on the excitement, anxieties and profound interests of the child — since I began reading Sylvia Ashton-Warner in the early 1960s.[101] When teaching reading, a teacher using Ashton-Warner's method gives the child the right (hot) word, one that will be learned at one glance and stay with the child. The teacher has found the caption for the child's hot *intention* (and used it to move the child another step toward literacy).

As we observe the children we often discover that our original questions weren't the important ones; the children are sparked by quite different matters, important to them and the stars they navigate by. We need to keep revisiting our assumptions, adjusting what we believed and re-framing our questions so they will refer to what we see and hear the children doing. We take these best ideas to the children, observe their interest or lack of it, tinker with what we brought until they come aboard or we decide to abandon them. C. G. Jung has a name, "obedience to awareness"[102] for processes such as bringing *our planning* into harmonious agreement with *the children's interest*. Most ideas we bring to children, what we say, what we ask them to do, must be inquiries into *their* ideas, rarely signals about what's important to *us*.

---

101.   See my book, *Pay Attention to the Children: Lessons for Teachers and Parents from Sylvia Ashton-Warner*. You can order it from: *www.eceteacher.org*

102.   I can't find a particular source for this comment. I first heard it in the Jung films.

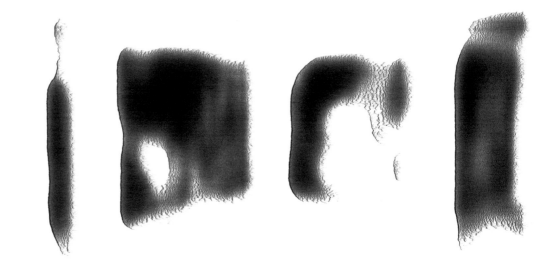

Elsewhere in this book we talk about projects documented and published in Reggio Emilia. In each instance, children's intentions were realized in wonderful ways, because the adults had helped them fulfill their interests and discover how capable they were, and what skilled work they could do.

Reading documentation of these projects raises the standards we set for ourselves, and opens us to doing amazing things with children.

Planned or spontaneous?
The fluid quality of working in the Reggio way

It is important for pedagogy not to be the prisoner of too much certainty, but instead to be aware of both the relativity of its powers and the difficulties of translating its ideals into practice.
— Loris Malaguzzi[103]

Dr. Malaguzzi's advice here is critical to understanding our work. If we become certain of anything, we stop inquiring about what it is. *Certainty puts an end to questioning, listening and looking more closely.*

If we stop paying attention to what's really happening, we won't provide the children with what *they* require, instead we'll hand them what *we* think will be good for them, reverting to, and trapping ourselves in adult-focused pedagogy. Children rarely step up to ask, in words, for what they want.

We need to learn to be *safe and comfortable in uncertainty*, a challenge for most of us, since we tend to want to control. After all, we've been rewarded all our lives for being certain, for knowing right answers!

Lesson plans

Does the staff make daily or weekly lesson plans in a Reggio-inspired classroom? If so, how is planning done? Does one follow a basic format?

Conventional lesson planning is a device for permitting a supervisor to know what will happen in the future in your classroom. This works well when it delineates pages to be read, writing assignments to be written, math problems to solve or songs to learn. It works poorly if the teacher intends to be responsive to the children, the mood, the weather, the news — the living classroom realities of children and teachers on a given day. In the US in recent years, most teachers write a plan and then, controlled by it, stick to it as closely as they can.

---

103. In Edwards, C., *The Hundred Languages of Children* (1st edition, 1993)

It will show how we will collaborate with other adults. Both the atelierista's and the teacher's viewpoints will inform what we share. With this kind of thinking, the teacher and child co-construct their thinking, questions and work.

Documentation allows the children to return to the time of the experience, and revisiting allows them to consider it in depth, and from different points of view. As I show them photos or video of what they have done and listen to their ideas, I speculate, interpret and frame what might come next, staying closely aligned with the work the children actually produce. This documentation process leads to a dynamic and fluid curriculum, emerging from what the children do and say.

As Dr. Malaguzzi reminds us, "Stand aside for a while and leave room for learning, observe carefully what children do and then, if you have understood well, perhaps teaching will be different from before."[104] ❧

104. From Edwards, C. *The Hundred Languages of Children 1993*

Too many questions

Early in this journey it is natural to ask "How do you implement this? What is the documentation process? How do we come to re-imagine the child? How do we change our current practices? How do we work with families in this new way?" We hope others will tell us. Given time, we come to realize it is about the transformations we make, as we learn to live with uncertainty, responding to what is really going on now, not just plugging in generalized, textbook solutions.

How can we make our teaching reflect our beliefs? It's difficult to describe this work to others because each individual's journey is different. Our strengths vary. Many resist the discipline of the documentation process — of thinking based on observation. Many resist collaboration. Sometimes, when it's hard, we want to go back and depend on the cookbook. Teaching informed by Reggio thinking is authentic and passionate teaching, illuminated by our vision of good lives in good communities. For each of us it is a struggle to find ways of relating to children that respect them and help them grow well.

Dr. Malaguzzi told us, "Don't become the prisoner of certainty." An old Chinese proverb is: "To be uncertain is uncomfortable, but to be certain is ridiculous." ໖

We have always felt relief when we learned to do something "the one right way."

But it's a false relief, a mirage based on generalizations that often fail. Instead we must listen to Dr. Malaguzzi, who teaches us that to be certain is to be trapped.

The work of becoming a mindful teacher involves abandoning quick fixes, standard responses, or doing things only one way.

Healing our hurts

The people of Reggio developed their educational approach in response to the ravages of World War II. It is integral to their way of life. For many of us this kind of teaching has come to mean something similar — healing our hurts and reviving our teaching lives so we become good for children, just as we hoped to be when we entered the field of teaching.

There can be no keener revelation of a society's soul than the way in which it treats its children.
—Nelson Mandela

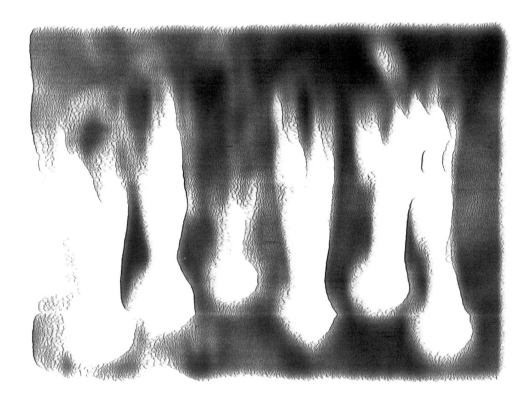

CHAPTER 27
The Race for Everyone! project
Note: All photos in this chapter are by Marie Catrett

Vivian Paley's quotation reveals where our way of designing routines originates: in our curiosity and in the children's. The process of our research starts with an idea. We need to be sure to try it at the right time with the right children, to consider it with our colleagues and refine it, so it becomes a good, useful routine designed to support strong, competent children.

Let's revisit Marie Catrett's home childcare program, *Tigerlily*. You met Marie and the six children she teaches in Chapter 13, when they went to the train station.

A new project emerged when the children noticed Marie training for months before running a half-marathon. She brought a map of the race to Tigerlily. She proudly finished the race, and like everyone who finished, she got a medal.

From her 1/15/13 documentation:

My running has been a topic of conversation with the children. They know my orange shoes are for running fast and that I was practicing to run in a race 1/13/13. On Friday kids made cakes for me in the sandbox so I could make wishes, blow out candles, and have good luck in the race. They speculated:

Willa: Will you get a medal when you run the race?

Marie: Yes! Everyone who finishes gets to have a medal.

Willa: If you get a medal will you wear it to school on Monday so I can see it?

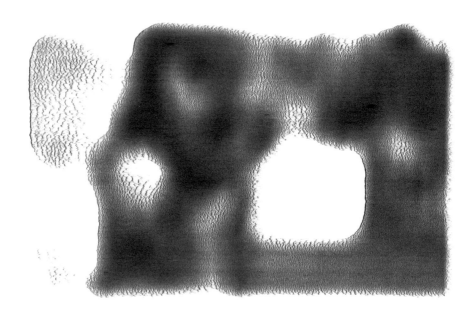

1/15/13

Marie: So here's what I wanted to say. We've been looking at the map that I used for my race, and I'm thinking that maybe we want to plan a special day to have a race at school.

Willa: Well yeah, but how? Would we get some medals to give everybody?

Daphne: Yeah, we'd have to get medals!

Much, much excited talk about "getting medals..."

I then do some hurrying-it-along adult business and say "I knew how to do my race because I had a map. Maybe we could make a map of my street if we were going to have a race on it. Now, of course, I can see how we could have stayed in the kids' thinking around medals in that conversation and taken tiiiiiime there, yes? The kids could have come up with, perhaps at some point, run on Marie's street? I did it for them, though quickly it got picked up.

Marie and I processed what was raised in this documentation, separately and together. There was material about the need for some of the children to win, which we've left out for privacy reasons. There could have been time to talk about what medals mean, and why a map was needed, but all of this came in a rush, as it sometimes does when we're with children and all of us are excited. We still are learning from the Reggiani how to start a project slowly, and to slowly pick out the important elements to give greater focus.

1/15/13 (continued)
Daphne: Maybe we could run all the way to your mailbox and then back.

Willa: Maybe all the way to the tallest pole and back.

Marie: Is the tallest pole on my street?

Willa: Uh huh.

Daphne: And then all the way back to your house and we can get a medal! Yeah, I want Willa to run and me to run and Wyatt and Elias and Emerson.

Willa: And Nayeli. [Nayeli was not at school that day.]

Wyatt: And I'll help Elias run, 'k?

Co-mentoring

It was decided that the children would have a race. Shortly thereafter all kinds of questions arose and Marie included me and our colleague, Nicole Mitchell, in her collaboration:

- How to connect this activity to the children's ongoing interest in maps and map-making.

- How to prevent those children who insist on winning or being first from either dominating the activity or descending into grief.

- How many adults would be needed for adequate supervision on a city sidewalk.

- What kinds and colors of medals would the children make?

- What was a logical, good order for all these stages of this important project to proceed?

The "I win" factor

Marie held discussions about the "who wins the race" question with the children, and *most of them* liked a solution where "we all win". There was at least one child who had deep reservations about this idea, who wanted to be the only winner. Later that child came to enjoy everyone's pleasure in winning.

The children make medals

1/22/13   Marie: Say about winning?

Daphne: That means we get a medal.

Willa: How about we make the medals?

Wyatt examines Marie's medal

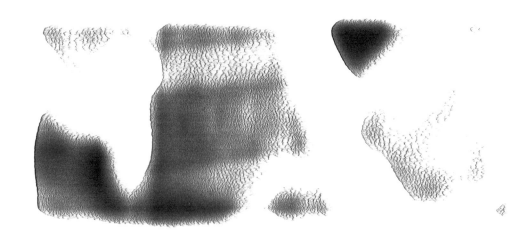
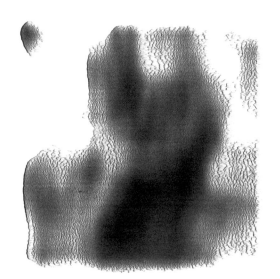

Daphne: My map about the run. These are the cones and that's the sidewalk I run.

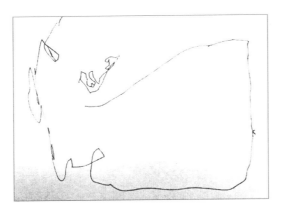

Willa (tracing with her finger, notice her U shape is just like the path our feet made today!) Shhhh-hhhhhhhhhhooooo (her noise for "fast") Like this, like this, to the finish line. (Small figure near middle top of page) That's the waiting spot. The hill that is your driveway.

Emerson (with the building blocks, his favorite medium!): This is the starting line (left), this is the finish line (right). It is a race!

We adults discover the need to practice the race

We all realized there needed to be a *practice race* or two so that the children's map-making could connect to their *experience* and their maps become representative of reality rather than of fantasy (see Vygotsky and Velcro™, *page 51*) As a longtime teacher of four-year-olds (Marie is new to this age group, but very experienced and a whiz at two-year-olds) I knew that only some of her children were ready to accurately represent the race route, but that after they had physically experienced the route, more would be ready to draw it quite clearly.

Nicole had this to say:

I would love to see Marie's reflection on this paragraph. I remember us sorting through this and the true hypothesis building that took place. Genuine puzzlement over how to guide the children deeper into more intentional, accurate representation characterized the thinking we all brought to the table. This felt close to what I imagine is Reggio collaboration — the teachers "sifting" through many pieces in order to find the "rocks" that can be used to build the foundation for growing project work. Our conversation was theoretical (what are the children *thinking, feeling, REALLY interested in here*) as well as practical (what days to practice, how to pace it, types of medals, etc.) and this was most fulfilling — bridging these elements so that they align and highlight the purpose and logistics. This is rarely easy and it seemed to come together well throughout our conversation that day!

in as a group, but wouldn't one-at-a-time be better? I felt like kids did know their name was in there — but how awful if they didn't! Nayeli, who ran last, did say to me, as she looked at one more paper in the hat, 'well, that just has to be my name'."

Everyone raced hearing the cheers he or she had planned, all the children cheering as instructed — and they returned indoors feeling great and with enough experience to make their better-informed maps. After reading my narrative, Marie responded: "Yes! Double yes, we did all return inside with very good hearts indeed." We were still somewhat puzzled by Nayeli's request for silence. It took several discussions to figure out that she was concerned for two things: one, she doesn't like loud sounds, and two, she was concerned that what was said should be genuine and authentic — a most remarkable and wonderful concern!

Go Elias, go!

I wonder what "silence" means to the kids.

Willa: Silence is when you don't make a sound forever.

Emerson: Silence means quiet. I like quiet because it is not loud.

Nayeli: Silence means cheering. (Moves her mouth open and shut but makes no sound). That's cheering to me.

Daphne: Silence means it isn't any fun.

Marie: Oh, I feel you Daphne. When I'm doing silence part of me wants to do something to show how glad I am and how excited…

The children make maps, part II

After the first practice race, four of the six children were able to do recognizable map-making. Those maps will continue to instruct or at least inform those who are not yet accurately representing in their drawings.

I asked, "Have you discussed with the children which of the maps they drew are helpful?" And I suggested, "Maybe 'I want to hang the maps on the wall that can help us think about the race.' I think you'll learn a great deal about the children's thinking from such a discussion."

Marie responded: "Yes! So, now, we have done this part. I expect to share the documentation on this more tomorrow. We did in fact hang one map picture each today. Daphne probably saw it and asked about it before I could bring it up. Several more maps were made today and I told them "these are practice maps we've begun. And when you make a map you think shows even better about the race, we'll put the even better one up in its place." Nayeli made another, really beautiful map again today."

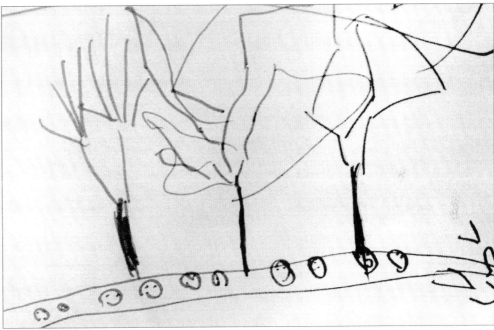
Nayeli's beautiful map

I love that *practice* has become a known idea in this group's culture. I wrote an article long ago about "editing" which, I now realize, was about *practice*.[105]

105. *ecrp.uiuc.edu* Volume 1 Number 1

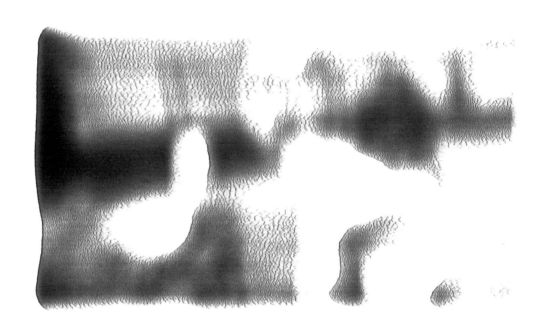

such good days in each other's company, our project is the ongoing story in which we take an ever more profound look into who we are and who we want to be together."

I observed the children, teachers, housekeeping staff and atelierista arrive in the morning, and greet each other. The children would play for a short while, and then the teachers and children would gather to plan the day. The adults had already had a short meeting to plan, and they announced events and appointments specific to the day, including ongoing project work. Some children made and kept only a few appointments, preferring basic, always available work: building with blocks, dressing up and doing dramatic play or climbing on indoor or outdoor structures.

You've got an appointment!

Leslie reports how this was working in her Honolulu classroom in 2009:

When, day after day, Miko didn't choose painting, we found ourselves in a quandary. We don't want to force an activity on a child, yet we believe in expanding and developing his acquisition of the hundred languages. We think children need many ways to express themselves, and Miko, so far, has Japanese, English and blocks as his only areas of competent expression. Asked to choose an activity, he plays it safe and doesn't choose to experiment or explore.

When I visited Reggio in 1999 I didn't get to observe the classroom meeting. When I asked how they organize their days, our hosts said, "We don't think in terms of schedules, we think, rather, about *appointments of the day:* what important appointments, necessary to their continuing work, are available to the children today?"

In the mornings, we teachers announce the appointments of the day. Each child draws his or her plans and appointments. Gigi and Steffi and Miko and all the others select where they want to work that day and then draw icons or symbols in their journals showing their plans and appointments of the day: time in the studio, minor field trips, blocks, dressing up, etc.

We especially want to hear from children who want to work in the studio, so we can make sure each one will have time there. Some children will return to work on some part of a project. Most children are eager to get their hands on the media we offer. But not Miko. He's building with blocks again. We like his skillful designs but we also want his horizons to expand.

Miko doesn't ever choose painting (or clay or wire) for himself. So sometimes we choose it for him. During this planning time we simply tell him he has a painting appointment. (Sydney tells me she used to say to the children, "Most of the time, you choose, but sometimes I choose.") Over time we will

exactly, but it seemed interminable) this incredibly patient teacher, who held fast to her conviction that children are capable of doing this, sat with a book poised in her hand and repeated, "This is where I am going to hold the book. I will wait for you to find a place where you can see and be comfortable."

That was all she said, with long pauses in between, giving the children a perfect problem-solving, critical-thinking opportunity. Eventually they figured it out. Within a week carpet squares and circle time were no longer a part of the classroom and I was changed forever!

The children discovered "I can move my own body to a place where I am comfortable and can see/participate." And "I can ask someone to move over so I can see better." Either way, it became the children's management concern, not the teacher's problem. Those who needed more language got it from the grownups. "Here is a place for someone." "Sometimes I say such-and-such when someone is bothering me."

In the classroom where Holly Koehler modeled and advocated daily for the children's capabilities, behavioral issues diminished dramatically. Children who had been silent for a year in another class now found their voices and asserted their rights. This transformation to an authentic learning community took time, patience and constant conversation among our staff and parents.

Now I am in the teacher position. I work with a team who do not yet understand this philosophy and instead work to control children. I am the advocate for the children's capabilities. I am the one repeatedly informing others that given time children will figure it out. My job is to model my expectation of problem-solving without demanding compliance.

Changing circle time

While reading about the Italian's reflections on their morning meetings and confronting my own dislike of American circle time, the difference between the two prompted me to re-think our meeting ritual.

so — we got rid of the old institutional schedule! Instead, we have tailored the day to our culture and our classroom community.

When my director asked me why I eliminated circle time, I explained the thinking which had led me to try the new schedule. This satisfied her and later, too, the NAEYC accreditation validator. Revising the way we organized our day so as to suit our classroom community enriched the dialogues and friendships among the children. We're living authentically and building rich memories! We don't miss our old circle time a bit! ॐ

that these adults know the children very, very well, since they stay together for three years in a community where there's a lot of reflection, dialogue, and documentation. Perhaps the reason I worry about this occasional interference is cultural.

Another kind of help is portrayed in the scene toward the end of the video *To Make a Portrait of a Lion*[107] at the celebration of their project, where the children are going to act out being a lion, and they're preparing a costume, gluing a mane on a Styrofoam™ lion's head. The atelierista sees how slowly the work is going, and shows them a much better way. The children finish up efficiently, and the playing — which was the point — now can begin.

Here in North America, we generally believe that children's work should be their own. In Reggio Emilia there's much more of a sense of *we* than there is in the U.S. In Italy the emphasis is often on *our* work rather than what *one child* can do alone. Adults there base their judgment on long-term, intimate knowledge of the children, and usually their judgment is accurate.

In the U.S., since we generally don't stay with a group of children for three years and we're usually not as intimately connected with the children, we must consciously consider when and why we give children assistance. We must be sure to know *why we're intruding on a child* — and it almost always is an intrusion. This is a specific case of the general rule: *Don't do anything unless you know why you're doing it.*

We go into any teaching situation with too little information — about the children, or the day's energy, or the parents' anxieties — yet we must do something today with the children, despite knowing as little as we do. We'll only know more after we observe and consider our observations about who these children are and what they care about.

This seems to be a good place to repeat what Dr. Malaguzzi urges:

> *It is important for pedagogy not to be the prisoner of too much certainty, but instead to be aware of both the relativity of its powers and the difficulties of translating its ideals into practice.*

He's telling us to hold *very tentatively* onto what we decide in advance to do with the children (that is, we shouldn't necessarily *follow* our lesson plans). If we're too certain that we're on the right path, too fixed on our one plan, *we will miss important signals children are sending us,* signals that would lead to alternative, more authentic teaching and learning paths.

---

107. Available in the USA from Reggio Children. *http://zerosei.comune.re.it/inter/pubs/audiovideo.htm*

CHAPTER 30
About provocation

A provocation is a portal inviting you deeper. It's an idea or question that carries us further into the subject. In the train story[108] Marie took the children to the station to provoke Elias to broaden his experience of trains and his relationships with the other children.

Provocation can bring the children to a place where they see that there is more to be explored, depth or breadth they hadn't yet seen. With well-thought-out provocative language we move them to the vicinity where they can explore further and respond more profoundly. New languages, new materials and surprises can provoke new thinking.

Sometimes no provocation is needed, yet *considering* possible provocations can assist you in further planning after you've observed the children and talked with your colleagues. If finding out about Reggio work has made you think that you've been teaching children in a superficial way, learning to provoke deeper thinking will help your teaching become more profound. A good start is to consider the question: "How am I going to open up this subject so it will be most productive?" The resulting provocation is what you'll use to help yourself and the children enter more complex territory. (In this context, you might want to reread the Race for Everyone! in Chapter 27.)

If four-year-old Anthony's experience has only been in a wading pool and we take him to a swimming pool he will respond differently. He can think about going into water in a new way. I took Anthony across the George Washington Bridge later, when he was six, after we had spent time together in my class and in wading pools and in swimming pools. I was still surprised, when, from the car, he noticed the water beneath us — the Hudson River — and

---

108. See *page 100*

CHAPTER 31
It depends: Specifics

When we say "It depends" that's shorthand for "It depends on the *specific situation or context*."

When facilitating a workshop I try never to respond to questions that begin "My daughter always...."or "The children in my class never..." Instead, as I did with the father whose son bit him[110], I reroute general concerns to uncover *specifics*:

- Who?
- Where?
- When? What was happening just before this?
- How did you respond?
- What happened then?
- How long since he'd eaten?
- What were the other children doing?
- What's the usual story children tell about this child?

We can learn only from specifics, not from generalities. We need to look at what Janey might be trying to do, and imagine other particular ways of satisfying her particular intentions. Then we can begin to help her unpack her issues and discover better routes to her goals.

Active listening requires that the listener insist that the person who is describing a situation pay attention to the detail — like showing us a movie, one frame at a time. "It depends" means to me that I can begin to help *only* when

---

110. See *page 198*

CHAPTER 32
Baby Talk: Stress-free conversations with babies & toddlers

This bit of advice is for people who are going to start talking with babies and toddlers: childcare workers, au pairs, parents-to-be or foster parents, teachers and families. A baby, though small, is a real person, capable of initiating communication and responding to it from early, early on. This conversation won't use adult vocabulary, and it can be with or without words, just as it is with older children and adults.

Babies pay close attention! They scan the world seriously, looking for cues and connections. Infants and toddlers learn to trust their own ability to communicate when we observe and listen and respond in ways that let them know their communications are recognized, heard and valued. Your adult joy is to share the pleasure of back and forth conversation, to wait for responses from babies, helping them learn that verbal and nonverbal communication are the bridges that connect people. No tests, no challenges, no showing off are needed, but rather simple dialogue, exchanging with each other with attention and respect.

I call this story:

"What's that letter? Who's the President?

What's this color?"

In 2007 the parents of Felicia, an eighteen-month toddler, introduced me to their child. They were in their early 40s, highly educated, devout, well-to-do parents, clearly in love with their child, and proud as they could be. The child's uncle and I had arrived just after ten in the evening. I had never met this family before, but I was scheduled to stay with them while I did some

Alternatively …

If we're not showing off Felicia's ability to name things and speak clearly, if we're not focused on showing others how smart she is, how should we relate to her?

I like to meet toddlers differently. I like to sit down on a low chair or the floor, and open my arms and legs. The child notices me, checks me out, and when she is ready, when she has decided I'm interesting, she finally approaches. I ask even an infant in arms, "May I hold you? (I don't expect an answer, but some form of conversation does take place — an exchange with each of us using the language tools we have developed so far). I keep our interaction very gentle, trusting the child's interest in the world and her curiosity to establish our relationship, without my making demands. I particularly avoid controlling hugs, tackling, tickling or rough bouncing. And testing questions!

What might you say to an infant or a child? Listen to skilled baby-people.

- Sportscast. Report, play-by-play what the baby's looking at, and your thinking about what he or she might want from the environment.

    "You're looking at the tree. You like to see the leaves move."

    "You're interested in those children."

    "You're looking at the sandbox. I'll help you go there."

- Extend vocabulary.

    "Ba? You'd like me to throw you the ball?"

    "Yes, you've got some peanut butter on your elbow."

- Word Play.

    "You've got your toes in the squishy, splishy mud."

    "Jennifer, Jennister, Guinevere. You are so lovely!"

    Follow the lead of the child

    "What do you see? Is it that bug?"

    "You'd like to go to those children? I'll go with you."

- And don't ask questions to which you already know the answer!

CHAPTER 33
Assessment (without testing)

Tests don't make children smarter, don't make schools better, and don't inform parents and the community about the children in ways that are productive. They are frightening, and worse, preparing for tests takes valuable time away from a fluid schedule and authentic teaching and learning, diminishing both the test-taker and the test-giver.[111]

Children younger than those in grade 1 have historically escaped testing, but nowadays, as private schools administer tests to screen preschoolers for entrance to kindergarten, or even for entrance to preschool, the danger threatens younger and younger children.

Below, Leslie describes how a skilled teacher finds out what a child knows without testing:

I don't drill children on colors or shapes but as the teacher I do need to know what the child in my care knows and have some understanding of how he thinks. I need to know the details: Is he right- or left-handed? Does he grip a pencil as if it weighed ten pounds or hold it gently? Does he look at books? How does he hold a book, turn pages, or read (or pretend-read) aloud? To learn this I don't have to set up a test and have the children respond to uniform questions. Instead, I make time when I can observe and note what children can and cannot do.

Bennet arrived at our school identified with speech difficulties. He made remarkable progress. As his speech grew clearer we realized he was a very competent learner. I wanted him to find kindergarten comfortable the following year, and I knew that kindergarten teachers like children to be able to name

---

111. Subscribe to Susan Ohanian's newsletters for excellent continuing information on testing and other school issues. *www.susanohanian.org*

When we meet the children authentically, align with them, and let them lead us in play, we can discover and plan any lessons they need. This way we can accomplish assessments without sacrificing relationship, courtesy, or joy. ❧

More about what we do instead of testing

Instead of testing Bennet, Leslie is mindful, noticing that Bennet is proficient in all his colors except grey, but also knowing why, during the following week, she pulled Bennet and a few others into a small group for a lesson exploring how gray and how it affects the colors that border it. *It's crucial for teachers to know, as Leslie does, why they're doing what they're doing*, and it's also important that supervisors *insist that teachers know the reasons* for what they do.

If we don't know the reasons for what we do with children we can't provide good curricula. Without understanding the underlying reasons, our observations and documentation will be shallow and lead to dead ends, defeating their purpose. In the absence of intention, our teaching will be superficial and cannot help the children take their thinking and their work to a deeper level.

Probably the most important element of this move away from testing is that parents learn more about how tests rarely help our teaching and the children's learning. Every human being is much bigger than any test that can be given!

what the child's goal is, I can usually offer him a way to get to it without upsetting the grownups around him. I do this without resorting to time out. The more I do it, the easier it gets.[113]

Time out is used to manage the classroom. But it's *not a teaching solution* — the child rarely learns from it. If we want children to learn *we'll have to enter the problem with them*, and find solutions together. We can't always do this from wisdom, and we may have to say things like: "Dana, I don't like what you did to Grant. Let's talk about it tomorrow, when we're both calmer." The incident is over, tomorrow is soon, and this evening you can get on the phone to your wisest friends or colleagues, learning how they would handle what Dana did *so as to help Dana grow, and importantly to support Grant.* That's much better than isolating a child who did something you didn't like!

Bad words

I think the "bad language" of children around age four is an exploration of power. "Stupid" or "dumdum" or racial epithets should be stopped, since they're weapons. I use my authority, telling children those words are used to hurt people and I don't want them used around me. As for four-letter words and the baby "bad words" (doodoo, caca) I think that the teacher who's deciding how to make them go away (and I think we'd all like to make them go away) needs to know how much of this language she can take and how she can remove the power from the words.

These words don't actually bother me, but I want to protect children from being punished or avoided or shamed for using them by people (adult and children) who are truly bothered by them.

I also know a bad word becomes much less bad if the teacher says it.

Here's what I do to strip power from the "bad" words. This is what suits me — but it may not suit you. Be authentic when communicating with children. So, for example, Paula comes to me with a complaint: "Jimmy said a bad word." I ask, "What word did Jimmy say?"

Paula either says "I'm not spozed to say that word" or, more likely, since I've given permission, she says "dumdum" or whatever the word was. If Paula won't repeat it, I ask Jimmy, who's usually glad to tell me, since that's how he exercises the power of the word. The rest of this conversation happens more or less publicly:

---

113. I describe this process in detail in *page 121.*

Leslie writes:

Early in my teaching, before I discovered Reggio thinking, a 4-year-old taught me much about life. Adam found out that language includes some words that others hear as offensive. I knew that Adam lived in the roughest neighborhood in the city and that his Dad had been in prison. I realized that these "bad" words might be helping Adam survive. For me to forbid them just because I found them offensive wouldn't have been right. How could I handle this?

One day Adam used the f word. Rather than punish him or say "We don't say that," I asked him why he said *fuck*, repeating the word (as Sydney recommends). He replied, "Well my Dad says it, and he's a big man."

Not wanting to judge anyone I simply said, "You are a young boy and when you get big like your Dad you can use that word. Ok?" He agreed and I never heard him say that word or any others like it again. ❧

In her example Leslie promises children that they will have the option to curse when they grow up. And of course, they will. As I said earlier, we'd all like to see these words disappear from our settings for young children. The question is, how do we do it: what is our image of the child? And what is our image of ourselves as teachers? Sometimes a strong word is damned handy!

Perhaps most important, I'd observe the wild play to figure out what it's about. What's underneath it? What kinds of fears and concerns are fuelling it? I'd try to create curriculum that would help children explore and diminish those fears or concerns. Observing, documenting, and working collaboratively with other adults to interpret what we see on the playground and in the classroom is useful for helping children, especially those children influenced by television violence or street violence, grow beyond repetitive, anxiety-induced, violent play.

Most adults with guns believe they have guns to *prevent harm* or for hunting. They don't expect to use the guns to attack others (except for hoodlums). Meeting with parents to inquire how they want their children to view guns can be a valuable discussion, allowing diverse opinions to be expressed, including your own.

I hope adults caring for young children are reading Nancy Carlsson-Paige and Diane Levin[114] on this subject. Their very thoughtful and provocative work on war play or violence among children deserves widespread attention. Perhaps you can ask parents to read some excerpts from their writing to provoke discussion on this topic.

114. These two authors are prolific and we suggest that you Google to find their latest work. Always good is *The War Play Dilemma*. Levin is the first author of this volume. Also see our Bibliography.

helping each other to understand the child. [116] There's no shortcut, just a process of uncovering who this child is, and helping her find comfortable ways to meet her needs.

116. See Forman, G. and Kushner, D. The Child's Construction of Knowledge.

the children it isn't ok when you're in charge, or that it frightens you." This is also the way I treat messy play, not allowing others to prohibit it so as to avoid the work involved in cleaning up, but doing that cleanup myself, because I believe in the importance and productivity of this play.

Why don't fours walk when they're indoors? Teachers tell them and tell them: "Don't run indoors," or "We *walk* indoors," but they simply don't. They aren't *aware of running*, but simply of moving or *going where they're going*. In my experience, making them aware of the people and things they can injure if they bump into them is more effective: "Please don't bump into anybody or anything" is a direction that makes more sense to most fours.

If your work is in an agency which won't permit you to relax control, at least imagine how you would monitor slides and running and such things differently if you had full responsibility. Some day you will.

An area in which rules tend to proliferate is the block corner. It is certainly reasonable to worry if children are using blocks as weapons in any way: throwing them or threatening to. The rule I often hear: "Only build as tall as you are" doesn't make sense to the children; they are doing something big and need to explore possibilities on a large scale. Building tall is satisfying, and so is making big crashes. Of course the children must be careful when doing either. Isn't the real rule: *Be thoughtful about blocks, because if they drop onto people they can hurt.* The way to make sure this guidance is always followed is to exercise your adult authority and close the block area immediately any time you see a serious infraction. I'd close it for the rest of the day, *without much discussion.* It's simple: we use the blocks properly or we don't use them. Once the block area has been closed because someone was being careless, the children who prize the blocks will start to insist that people playing there take good care of each other, becoming your allies: "Don't throw that or she'll close the blocks!"

By the way, foam rubber blocks are a terrible alternative. They're unstable and don't have enough weight to build with. I believe they were designed for teachers who don't trust children to behave sensibly — teachers who haven't learned that children *don't want* blocks falling on them, and can learn to handle them with respect.

Too small

Undersized outdoor equipment is very treacherous; it seduces children into doing things to challenge themselves, like climbing up and jumping off.

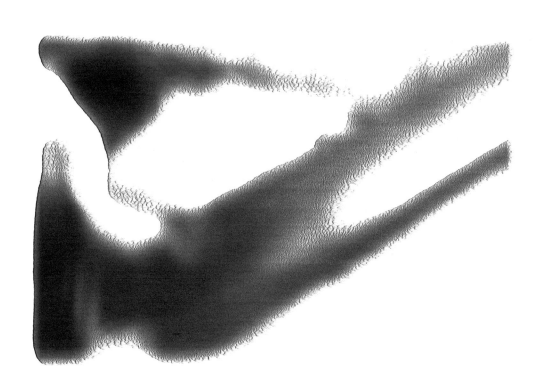

CHAPTER 38
Cleanup as collaboration

Leslie writes:

At the beginning of the school year, as I'm focused on building a disposition in the children to think about the community, I go to Marybeth at clean-up time and ask, "Do you need help? Would you like me to help you clean up?" If she says yes, and usually she will, I pitch in and we put away materials together. Another child often will join in and I tell Marybeth, "Great! Tommy wants to help you, Marybeth. Are the two of you OK cleaning up together?" Looking across the room, I see Suzie still has a lot of blocks to clean up, so I go help her. My message is about respecting each other and the community; *we all can help and we all do.*

Throughout the day I ask for help and one of the children volunteers. With other children in earshot, I thank my helper. I don't make a big deal of this; it's just part of my focus on relationship building.

Cleaning up a whole room seems overwhelming, so why not make it manageable in the child's mind? When things must be put away I ask the children to look around right where they are and put away the things that are close. When they finish I suggest "Please go see so-and-so, and give him a hand?"

Cleanup can be about building community and learning to pitch in. In the world beyond school there won't be someone who dims the lights as a signal to clean up, so I avoid this and other institutional rituals. However, people, young or old, can always look around and pitch in and help with tasks that are waiting.❧

the schools in Reggio notices the beauty (and the order) of the spaces. If children help create this order they can share in the pride it brings.

If you have beautiful things, it makes sense to ask the children to take good care of them. Order is contagious. If all the markers have caps, then when one is missing its cap we will quickly notice, and we can all look for it — but if we have some markers that are dried out and some that are missing caps, soon more will be lost or left uncapped. If we have dried-out markers because of left-off caps children will be discouraged from drawing. Where good systems are present people see them working, and we mostly want to follow them. We participate when we understand how we benefit. Neglect is another kind of system — a contagion to avoid.

Making the room beautiful to look at, with tools in their places, is seen by the Reggio Emilia community as part of the task of taking on the artists's perspective. Materials look best, work best and last longest when stored carefully. People like others who help them clean up. A beautifully arranged shelf is, itself, a work of art. Building a community is a fundamental Reggio way of thinking. As children replace materials in an ordered environment, it helps them construct ways of thinking about people and materials and encourages useful habits.

What kind of people are we growing here? Don't we want them to think about what's good for the planet and the species, as well as their families and themselves? Jonas Salk, the inventor of the polio vaccine, said, "If all the insects on earth disappeared, within fifty years all life on Earth would disappear. If all humans disappeared, within fifty years life on Earth would flourish as never before." Our routines, provocations and the few rules we make together must support children's creativity with good, organized materials if we want avert the kind of destruction predicted by Dr. Salk — if we want future generations to build an optimistic, healthy and imaginative world. We owe them that.

CHAPTER 39
The environment as the third educator

A child learns a great deal on his own outdoors. Photo: SGC.

Each classroom in Reggio Emilia is staffed with two teachers[119], and the Reggiani traditionally call the environment the "third teacher". Each school (usually three classrooms, one for 3's, one for 4's and one for 5's) has an *atelierista*, the artist who staffs the *atelier (art studio)*. There are many ways children learn without adult intervention when the environment has been prepared to interact instructively with them. Such a design has long been part of early childhood sciencing[120]. Magnets with various metal bits, funnels and waterwheels for water play, magnifiers and microscopes — all are teachers in this Reggio sense.

In Part VI we describe some ways we've watched the environment *teach*. We'll discuss North American uses of equipment we first saw used with children in Reggio. Then we'll explore some of the most important of the "Hundred Languages" that help people express themselves, and good ways of offering them to children. In Reggio Emilia classrooms materials are displayed so their nature is readily visible to all. These materials are stored within easy

119. More adults are added if "children with special rights" are in the group.
120. This word, "sciencing" became part of my vocabulary after I read the wonderful science textbook, *Teaching Elementary Science: Who's Afraid of Spiders?* by Selma Wassermann and J. W. George Ivany. Teachers College Press, 1996

CHAPTER 40
Artists and educators

The arts are fundamental resources through which the world is viewed, meaning is created, and the mind developed.
— Elliot W. Eisner, Professor of education and art, Stanford University.

We teachers tend to think in a linear, left-brained, language-dependent way. Artists are usually more right-brained and often think in images rather than words. Children need words *and* images for full expression of feelings and thoughts. Italian cultural tradition respects and embraces the positive tension caused by these contrasting approaches. Dr. Malaguzzi invited artists to join the program in Reggio to make use of their unique experience — to problematize and explore the differing perspectives and opinions that teachers and artists have. He wanted to explore and make use of those tensions, to deepen the adults' understanding of children, so they develop more complex and responsive ways to work with them.

Dr. Malaguzzi's intention in adding the atelier and atelierista (the art studio and the artist-teacher) was to create a place brimful with materials, colors, textures, ideas, thoughts, and controversies — to provide a sphere of creative friction, a domain not only *safe* and *supportive* for diverse views and a variety of approaches, but one which would also *provoke* them!

Thus, a substantial part of the excitement of the Reggio approach depends upon engagement between someone who speaks from the creative perspective and someone who speaks from the pedagogical perspective, both of them well informed about constructivist theory. When educated people from both camps listen closely to each other, avoid defensiveness, and engage in creative

The atelierista confers daily with the teachers and together they plan their appointments of the day with the children; S/he coordinates ways of helping the children think more visually and tangibly and creates lessons for those who need skills to more fully express themselves. As I see it, the atelierista has three main functions:

1. helping children realize their ideas in visual media.

2. offering children new techniques to broaden the children's ability to express themselves in various media.

3. coordinating and collaborating documentation efforts, and helping make them as attractive and accessible as possible.

The Italian ateliers differ from center to center. Just as each pair of teachers has a classroom which reflects their interests and style, and the children's, the atelier is the turf of the atelierista. It reflects his interests and style, and is where children do their larger and longer-term art works. Giovanni Piazza, for many years the atelierista at La Villetta School in Reggio, is fascinated with machines, and often, in his atelier, children constructed machines: Ferris wheels, aqueducts, and so forth. Mara Davoli[122], at Pablo Neruda School, is fascinated with design and color, and these themes recur in her atelier. Vea Vecchi, at Diana School, displayed famous works of art and architecture interspersed with the children's artwork on the walls of her studio, stimulating ideas and reflecting problems and solutions the children — like all artists — encounter in their art. She was fascinated by the theories the children constructed, and developed interesting and valuable ways to permit the children to explore the implications and possibilities of their theories.

The atelierista does much of the work of making documentation panels, taking photos, transcribing conversations, and thinking about the visual impact of the panels which convey and reveal the children's growth and their process. S/he collects data, organizes it, collaborates with other staff to see what it indicates for future activities, and sometimes offers it back to the community through panels or other displays. The classroom teachers participate (but to a lesser extent) in all of these tasks.

Jordan Guillory, the atelierista who works with Leslie in Hawai'i says:

> If the atelierista does not have training in the fine arts he should be steeped in the interdisciplinary arts and have actually done artwork himself so he knows how frustrating materials and

---

122. See my description of the black and white lesson I saw atelierista Mara Davoli teach when I was in Italy, on *page 252*.

After considering the implications of their work in clay, the children drew again, and these designs reflected the children's fresh "hands-on" knowledge — the lesson Giovanni had successfully provoked with his challenge! The children learned by doing — by making models, by their own practical efforts — rather than through words or lectures — and that is the gift of the atelier.

Children, encouraged, will construct theories, in turn developing their disposition to make *more* theories. In Reggio children are supported whenever they theorize, however inaccurately, and *are not given* "right answers." Reggio teachers *provoke* further investigation. They do not give children the correct answer, but instead *help them construct it*. Children in Pam Oken-Wright's Cat Project (in Richmond, Virginia) never came to agreement about whether the heart or the brain was the "boss of the body". For that matter, do we adults really know the answer? That question was left to be considered again later, at another stage of development. Supporters of each position *did* come to understand some of the reasons the others had for their position — a major step in critical thinking.

Children in Marie Catrett's *Race for Everyone!* were willing to give up the need to be the only winner in the face of the non-competitive solutions the children devised and implemented in response to the directive by the majority of the children that "everybody has to win."

In the Rain in the City project in Reggio Emilia, after their initial discussions, the children depicted what they'd found in their investigation of what is *in* and also *under* the city. Some children developed theories about God's role in bringing us rain, and others more or less reconstructed the rain cycle. These differing theories were left unresolved. During this study, the children made beautiful, thoughtful three-dimensional representations of their theories and discoveries with enthusiasm and care, using drawings, wire sculptures, models in plexiglass and wonderful straws and tubing (for pipes) and drawings of itty bitty rats.

Children's work in the studio isn't mainly about the product, but rather about the *process* (although the products are wonderful) — about thinking, expression, and problem-solving representation of ideas in diverse media. Their work connects the head to the hands and the hands to the heart, and brings a new mindfulness to both teachers' and children's work.

what is there; you'll miss seeing the children, learning.[124] You'll also miss the chance to ask the child about his thinking, as you look together at his work.

The atelierista needs to be process-focused, since the children are often more interested in the process than the product. A focus on representing our experience allows us to slow down the pace or rhythm of the day in order to become more of a planner. We adults do this through our documentation process, and the children with their representations of what they experience, think, and see. These representations work in parallel.

The studio brings children and adults together in small groups which permit teachers to dialogue and co-construct understandings with the children. This also allows for close and supportive relationships to develop among the children. The atelier is a place that leads to intimate discussions — a place where many possibilities are present, awaiting action.

The atelier helps us bring our new eyes into our thought processes. As Thoreau wrote: *"The question is not what you look at but what you see."*

A child builds with clown-shaped figures. He is expressing himself in a non-messy, flexible, medium. Photo: SGC

124. Wonderful set of examples of looking beyond the art can be found in *We are All Explorers*, (see bibliography) see especially *page 119*, called "Thinking about what is on a child's mind".

If we substitute a quick and efficient lesson learned from a conference sales-room demo for the open-ended experience of discovery and "messing about," we are all robbed of a deeper, richer understanding. Here's another occasion to allow the children to *take time* to play with the light table, allow them *time* to make discoveries, allow them to develop a range of ideas and uses. Otherwise we run the risk of *understanding too quickly*. We should be alert to avoid diminishing children's elaborate and profound ideas and theories. A light table isn't like a Monopoly™ board, to play on only with Monopoly pieces and rules — it's more like a magical tray on which you can put *anything that will fit, and there are no rules!*

An environmental teacher

A colleague asked me why I needed a light table. "I could just hold the work up against the window when the sun comes in, and get the same result," she said. I replied, "Yes, of course one could, but that would only occur when the teacher thought about it, and not *whenever the children use it*. The light table can *continuously and passively* support the children's creativity; expand their understanding of dark and light and of translucency, freeing time for me to teach other things." With the table giving feedback, the children construct their own theories and understandings of translucency. As they come to invent more and more possibilities, they will use the table more and more collaboratively and creatively.

Possibilities

During my week at Diana school I saw children watercolor and do collage at the light table there. A vase with flowers in water had been supplied as a possible model. In my own classroom some children preferred doing *everything* at the light table, but if the table was crowded, a child who didn't require the light as part of what he was doing would give his place to one for whom the light was necessary.

Every day, as they arrived in the morning the children in my first grade class signed in on an oaktag signup sheet (opaque) located on the light table. Then they made name-tag stickers (translucent), decorating them — usually with markers — in wonderful ways. Later in the day they built with Legos™ on the light table, and also traced things. Daily, they continued to create new uses for it. In this way the light table became a specialized teacher of translucency, always present in the room.

When I visited Rowanberry School in Portland, OR, children were drawing with their fingers in sand on the light table. Not only was this fun, but so

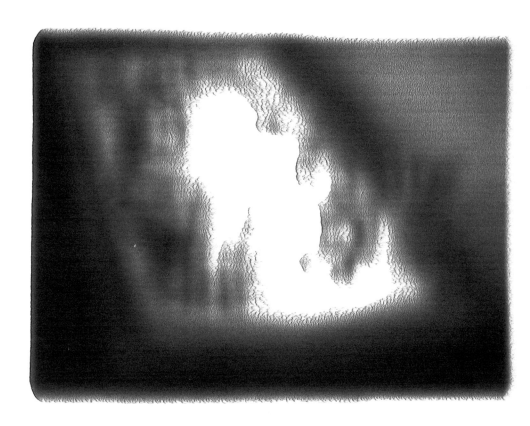

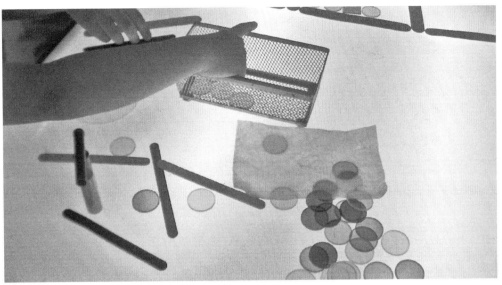

This work calls for a delicate touch. Photo: LG

Alvin arrived at the light table and briefly arranged and rearranged some tongue depressors he found there. As I began to take photographs, Kitty joined him. Alvin left soon afterwards, but Kitty added some other materials.

At first Kitty began arranging tongue depressors into squares, rectangles, letters, and other familiar shapes. Like many other children, Kitty has been taught only to give right answers, to please her parents by learning the alphabet, colors and shapes, and to stick with conventional, convergent thinking. I see my job as opening her imagination, and letting her experience the wonder of creativity and learning. I can imagine her new power, making choices about what she will put into her assemblages, and her capacity to create something close to what she had in mind.

Wanting to push her to freer expression, I encouraged her to walk around our classroom to find more things to play with at the light table. Experimenting with a wide range of opaque, transparent, and translucent objects, she opened her explorations to random and unknown configurations, and after ten minutes, invited me to play, too. "Ms. Leslie, you want to do this with me?" I sat down and began to play. Kitty would lead for a while, arranging objects on the table, and I'd copy her. Then I would start a new design, and Kitty would follow. Sometimes there was no leader, as we each made our own arrangement of materials and light. She searched the room for materials to add to the display, and so did I.

I fetched a ribbon spool out of the basket of plastic recyclables. In turn she went to get some transparent disks, and we began to move these around the light table. Then I opened a pair of scissors wide, and lay them flat, and she collected several more pairs of scissors, arranging them in a pattern around

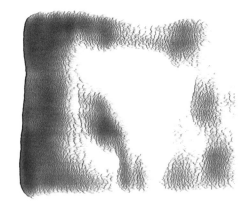

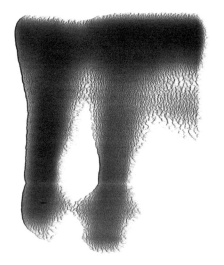

documentation panel now serves as a provocation for other children to explore the light table.꙱

Platforms for blocks and seating

Like the light table and Kaleidoscope, the block platform teaches us all to observe closely. You might ask yourself: Is it necessary that blocks be put away each evening? Why? Whose idea was that? What do the children gain from leaving them up? Putting them away?

I took this photo in Reggio Emilia in 1992.

In Reggio the platforms are about one meter square and about chest high for a child sitting on the floor. They function as small stages for blocks. Because the blocks are off the floor, custodians don't resist allowing block structures to stay up overnight (or for weeks or months). This permits a different kind of play — now children are moving and improving their constructions, editing them rather than just building, demolishing, and rebuilding. Instead of *here today, gone tomorrow*, there's development of ongoing design and elaboration of ideas. The children experience not only immediate gratification, but the possibilities more time allows.

Providing platforms for your classroom can define spaces for building with blocks or other materials. The surfaces of the platforms are carpeted, which allows children to lean the blocks against each other without the blocks slipping, falling or sliding — keeping noise down. Children either sit on the floor to manipulate materials on the platforms or (depending on what's going on) they may get up on the platforms themselves.

Platforms bring the building surface closer to eye level for the children, allowing them another perspective on what they are building. If you locate your platform next to a mirrored wall or, even better, in a mirrored corner, the children can see behind their work and can be continuously informed and provoked by those views.

Platforms can also be arranged in configurations to define areas in the classroom. I asked Pam Oken-Wright, for more information about the very large blocks that define her meeting space. Here's her reply:

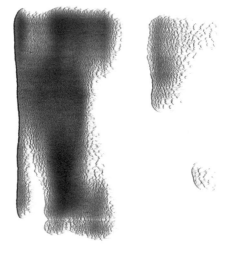

their ideas, the possibility of continuing tomorrow or later in the week what one couldn't finish today, uninterrupted time (no specialists taking children away at the wrong moment) — the better you organize the Environment as Educator, the more you'll know how to prepare for and permit her free rein; extra, expert staff at little or no extra cost!

This child has used pattern blocks to make a wonderful representation of BART, our San Francisco light rail system, 1973.

so people can view it without distraction. Decorations worth hanging should have some *connection* to the children.

That afternoon our new chairs arrived. It made a startling difference to have wooden chairs replace the jazzy, primary-colored plastic ones. When my supervisor, BB, next came to school, she wondered about the change:

> BB: Is this classroom look purposeful? My first reaction makes me think of children being forced to sit. I am surprised you chose them because they give the room a classroom look.

> LG: I think when you see the children in them you will see that the chairs are not so classroom-ish. Let me tell you a few of my considerations:

The environment is our "third teacher" and sets a tone for the children, parents and visitors. The old chairs projected an image of a child who needs stimulation, is motivated by bright colors, and needs to be separated from other children by high sides. The eye was drawn away from the work-place by the colored chairs. They didn't project our strong Image of the Child or the serious and important work the children do. The new chairs look a bit stodgy, but they are calm and neutral. The natural wood conveys a promise of serious work and play. With the neutral chairs, color arrives in the room in the children's sparkling eyes, their clothing, and in their works of art. We don't like those "nursery rugs" with busy letters and numbers and other pictures for the same reason — they pull attention away from the children. Just as a painter's studio is white or neutral, allowing the artist to deliver her vital choices of color, our children create *their own color* and artistry in their neutral work/play space.

The high sides of the cube chairs impede relationships. When a child is in the cube he is walled off from the child in the next chair. In contrast, two children can cuddle next to the teacher or each other on our computer bench. That intimacy was impossible in the cube chairs, but the new chairs permit it.

I've repeatedly observed the children putting three wooden chairs side-by-side to form a kind of bench. Seated together, the children lean into each other's space — and a wonderful connection is created. Sometimes you can see the children hugging or wrapping an arm around the child beside them. It's beautiful! Thus, our new chairs without arms.

CHAPTER 43
The Vocabulary Project

The Reggio Emilia word book

In the *Vocabolario Project* Mara Davoli, at Pablo Neruda School in Reggio Emilia helped children identify *words they liked* beginning with each letter of the alphabet, and arranged them in a book about words. The children drew beautiful "illuminated" letters to start each section, and offered sentences for their wonderful words.

CHAPTER 44
Playing in the metaphor

One Reggio project began with the children's fascination with puddles and led to a lengthy investigation of a particular puddle. As we read and look at the photos from the exhibit[126] the story unfolds:

Once upon a time there were some children, who were, like almost all Children, surrounded by rules — spoken rules, unspoken rules, controlling rules, benign rules — but rules, nonetheless. One of the classic rules for children has always been: "You mustn't step in puddles." Of course this prohibition makes the puddles even more attractive to the children.

Their teachers made a plan, and so one day, after a rain, the children and their teachers all put on their boots and went with their sketchpads to look at puddles. The teachers listened closely to what the children reported: "I can see some children in the puddle, but not others." Allesandro said he could see Marko in the puddle, but Marko was annoyed because he couldn't see Allesandro. The children commented as they drew, learning to look closely at the puddles. The teachers wrote down their comments.

Mostly, the children noticed that things in the puddle looked upside-down, opposite to the real world. This puzzled them and provoked a lot of discussion and play.

These discussions and games continued at school over several weeks during a rainy season. Their teachers provided puddle-shaped mirrors for the classroom floor, to remind children of wet puddles on dry days. This caused

---

126. See *The Hundred Languages of Children*, the catalog of the 100 Languages exhibit.

It's good and useful for adults to help the children construct their understanding of the purpose of rules; to help them understand why we embrace being right-side-up, driving on the legally approved side of the road, eating when hungry. Compliance with sensible rules is easier after you've tried living in the puddle.

Here's what Toni wrote:

Some Good Daily Practices to Keep You and the Children Ready for Special Challenges

- Don't hesitate to ask when you need help. Identify people who can be of help to you in your teaching, both in and out of our field, with both theory to underpin your practice and with practical solutions.

- As they arise, validate children's creative, different approaches to painting: scratching, flicking, spattering, and fingerpainting (even at the easel). We found this came in handy when children tried to represent the disaster of September 11th.

- Invite children who have expressed an idea to portray it again (and again) in a second (and third) medium. When you exhibit these works together children will feel deeply validated in their expression and parents will be more informed about the complexity of their children's thinking and feelings.

- Sit down, relax, and use a soft, slow voice when talking with a child about his artwork. Make time to do this even if you feel hurried.

- Stay neutral when reopening a discussion with a child after some time has passed, creating in your teaching voice a possibility without a demand.

- Provide children open access to unstructured art materials every day so they can express themselves (Pile 1973; Clemens 1991).

- Keep in mind that children are very often finely tuned to each other's thoughts and artwork. Expect, and look for, work that spins off other children's art and stories. Notice how art and play facilitate supportive relationships and contribute to a general feeling of acceptance and safety in the classroom. Show the children that their classmates honor their work.

- Support free expression and disclosure at all times. Children take their cues from you about whether or not a topic can be discussed openly in their center or school. We adults should always be on the side of children saying what's on their minds.

- Wonder and check to see if there are more meanings beneath the first explanations that children tell you as they label their artwork. Use neutral, open-ended questions to elicit deeper talk about artwork. At first you might say, "What's happening in this picture?" This allows a child to choose to describe the colors she mixed, the shapes she made, the journey she took, or the object or person she represented. Following that, you can ask, "Can you tell me more?"

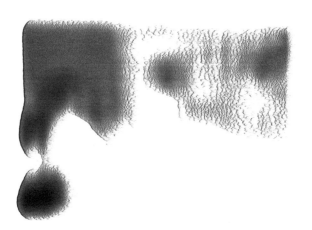

employed discarded materials. I saw another such curtain being made by the children out of little translucent plastic bits. Such work builds a sense of community. This kind of work transforms bits into beats of beautiful rhythm. It's useful for repurposing shiny discards and recyclables, and mingles the work of the more gifted artists with that of the less gifted, making everyone a participant in creating "something beautiful we made together".

Connecting literacy and arts education

A child who has become comfortable expressing herself in one language is more comfortable with languages in general. A child who has learned to read and write in one language can learn the next one much more easily. Since English is a more difficult language to read and write than many others, it's often better for a bilingual child to learn to read and write first in the *other, simpler to learn* language, for example Spanish, which is phonetically regular, before attempting to read and write in English.

A child who has represented her experience in one symbol set (i.e. drawing) is more comfortable with other sets of symbols (i.e. painting, sculpting, and writing).

Four-year-olds draw people. Photo:SGC

A child who has interacted positively with the world, communicating in multiple ways (hundred languages) is more open to new interactions. Successful interactions create a comfort zone, allowing children to embrace new possibilities — after a while we learn to believe that *new experiences will become comfortable.*

It follows that a child who comfortably expresses her experiences and symbolizes her feelings in multiple languages (speech, drawing, music, clay work, painting) will be more open to understanding the symbolized, expressed languages of reading and writing.

I don't mean to justify arts education by saying it supports literacy, since it's clear to me that the arts justify themselves, but we can *use this connection to convince others* to see the immense value of the arts in our lives and the lives

Agency

We want children to develop and experience the understanding that one can set out to do something and then accomplish it. This belief is called *agency*. It's born in infancy, and should continue to empower us all through our lives, but many of the things people do to "civilize" or even to protect children undermine their agency. The arts cultivate agency, as children come to understand what a medium can do, and through practice, they are empowered to express themselves through it. If our children can develop a stronger sense of agency in the time they are with us, built on their experiences and the reminders that documentation gives them about those experiences, they will have something of profound importance and great personal satisfaction. As Luis Valdez said, "The future belongs to those who can imagine it".

Continuing access to media

Just as with spoken language, once the child has a basic vocabulary in any medium he very likely will want to use it. Familiarity breeds utilization. That's why we emphasize regular ongoing access for children to all the media that have been introduced; so that each child can use his medium of choice — instead of one selected by the teacher for use that day — and thus continue to put his thoughts, ideas and feelings into his favorite media, expressing himself and sharing with others. The role of the atelierista includes helping children become more skillful in media, through lessons like the one described above where Mara helped children look closely at figure and ground[128].

Reggio thinking encourages listening and observing to see that the materials are supporting the children's work and expression. If the children don't find a way to express themselves they will be shortchanged. As Ralph Waldo Emerson said, "What lies behind us and what lies before us are tiny matters compared to what lies within us." Many teachers offer another new "art experience" daily, instead of helping children become skilled and more able to say what they have to say in languages they have become skilled in and enjoy. Continuing novelty puts the children into a daily experience of incompetence. I think we need to educate adults who interact with children to respect the need to express oneself.

Are the materials available, visible, sufficient in number, are they being used, and are they easy to share? About two months into the school year (and every two months thereafter) at the busiest time of the day, when children are engaged in work all around the classroom, do a survey of your materials and space. It's valuable to ask: Is there an empty area? Is there crowding? Are

---

128. See Clemens "Art in the Classroom: A special part of every day." http://www.eceteacher.org/articles/art.htm

(574, working in woodcuts as well as sculpture and paint). You can find printmakers like Romare Bearden, African-American (11,000), (3,860,000) muralists like Diego Rivera, Mexican (13,400) and his disciple, American muralist Emmy Lou Packard (2,040), and other white artists, too, architects like Frank Lloyd Wright, of Welsh descent, and our favorite artist to show to children, because of his work with nature, Andy Goldsworthy, British, (216,000).

The images you find can be printed and closely examined by the children. Ink and photo paper are costly, but so are books, and the choices of what to print (perhaps one a day?) can be made with children's participation... and so reflect their new interests, languages and understandings. Your artistry in teaching will help the children find the many forms of art that are waiting inside them to be expressed, bringing pleasure and satisfaction to the children, their families, and the rest of us, too.

When to give models

When the child has been unsuccessfully trying to do something, *this is the right time to offer help*. Let's take drawing an animal as an example. In Reggio, if a child is frustrated as he tries to draw or sculpt an animal, they give him a small plastic toy to examine and use as a model.[130] You can also go to Google Images and bring up multiple pictures which show that animal through many visions. "Does this look like what you were trying to make? Does this? Does this?" Our objective is to help the child do what she or he intends to do.

Our representations are often based on other representations. We don't have answers, but we can offer resources, saying, "This might help." We will see that Rodari taught children in Reggio Emilia that "stories are made of other stories".[131]

The point of art is to express the artist's ideas and feelings and to consider how we connect with ourselves and with other people.

Here is the poetic list children in Marie's group dictated. Wyatt was leaving to go to kindergarten, and on their last day of summer session they talked about what to do if you miss somebody.

Please notice how the children have come to understand deeply that the arts can help them deal with hard feelings:

---

130. See the photo on *page 196*
131. See Chapter 50

CHAPTER 46
Natural materials (and food)

Leslie writes:

An exhibit of Andy Goldsworthy's[132] work led me to think more deeply about how children might work with natural materials. I provided a container of polished stones for the children. As with blocks they repeatedly made satisfying constructions. The children went back to this day after day. These natural materials are familiar to some of the children and they bring their experience to them, and conversations about them. Working in groups they collaborated, building with stones.

Transitory artworks

Often teachers think of children's artwork mainly as something to send home to parents. Much of Andy Goldsworthy's art is ephemeral; it blows away, floats off, melts, dissolves, crumbles or is washed out to sea. We all have memories of making sand castles or mud pies in the backyard — work with a short lifespan. Today's children need more of that kind of play!

Don't play with food!

Teachers who bring foods into the classroom to use for crafts still hold the old, empty Image of the Child. What values do we communicate to children when we give them pudding and Jello™ to paint with? I think we offer mixed signals to children if we permit them to play with food at school, since "Don't play with your food!" is a rule in many, perhaps most, homes. Foods shouldn't be used as art materials. Some children still come to school hungry, and we mock their need when we offer food for play.

---

132. See *Rivers and Tides*, the video about Goldsworthy's work, Also see his wonderful coffee-table books. (You can sometimes find these expensive books second-hand. Don't miss them; they will interest and inspire the children.)

CHAPTER 47
Introducing clay: The ethnic material of our species

Clay is a special material; it's a language rich in form, function and connections. Children are usually very attracted to clay, provided that it is always given to them in *moist, pliable condition*. I cannot overemphasize this. Visiting classrooms I've often seen children abandon the dry clay their well-meaning teachers gave them. You will need to check the condition of your clay daily (this takes 15 seconds.) To avoid clay soup you will want to control how children add water to the clay. A good way is for each child to have a moist cloth or paper towel which he can squeeze to moisten his hands. If there's a spray bottle of water, it should be kept on a high shelf, and only sprayed by adults. Otherwise: clay soup.

Clay can connect children with many other people and cultures, both the living and the long dead. Pots, sculptures, and storage containers have all been made by hand since ancient times and can be visited in museums. Nowadays machine made clay products abound. Despite that, parents have long treasured a clay pin dish, a box or an animal or ashtray (no more ashtrays, please!) made by their child. Children love to make clay animals and characters from their favorite shows, books or fantasies.

The possibilities of clay are apparent to humans early in our lives. I've seen an eighteen-month-old child mold clay into a water-bowl for a plastic animal to drink from. We are privileged to introduce children to clay early in their lives, and allow them to explore its possibilities.

Dr. Malaguzzi wrote: "Our task, regarding creativity, is to help children climb their own mountains, as high as possible. No one can do more."

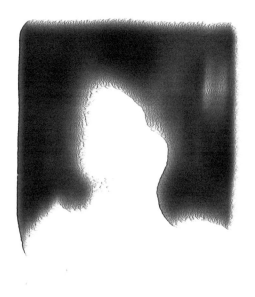

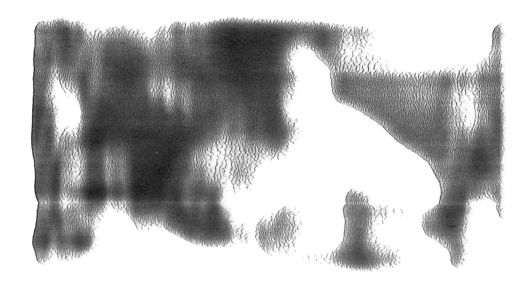

Please *hold back tools* for a long while, as much as three months in a full-time childcare program, and wait even longer if children are coming fewer than 40 hours a week. If you give tools now, *they* become the object of exploration — and we want the children to explore the clay! So we invite children to explore the medium using their fingers, palms, elbows, thumbs, and knuckles in many positions. After a few weeks, if they haven't invented them already, you can invite them to make a coil, or a slab, and then to add texture to the slab or build up a pot from a stack of coils. Some will spontaneously make nests and fill them with eggs and maybe even a bird. For a more detailed discussion see my favorite book on clay work, *Children, Clay and Sculpture*.[133] Eventually a child will have need for a tool — that's when we give him the tool that will help. We avoid giving tools too early because we want the child's experience of the clay to come directly, naturally and intimately through her fingers.

Clay shouldn't be given to children and then, after a day, a week, or a month, taken away from them. Keep this material *and any other basic materials you give the children* available *every day*, after you've introduced it.

Some children will make the same materials with clay repeatedly until they're ready to move on. Some learn from what other children are doing while others go inside themselves to find ideas to try. Children deserve your permission to repeat until they're ready to move on. Don't present clay in terms of the product we're going to make today: the tile, the pot made of coils, the vase, or the cup. When adults focus on products, show the children the steps to make the product, which is sometimes glazed and fired, and then taken home. A focus on product doesn't help children come to *understand* the medium — they have made it but they haven't internalized it. If there are products, they should come from the child's own intention and work, not an adult's list of what is to be learned or made.

When I took clay classes in my sixties I did a lot of work with my eyes closed — getting to know the clay was work for my hands more than for my eyes. Let each child establish her own relationship with the clay. Make it convenient to let children have clay again and again, every day if they want it. (Did I remind you to keep it moist and ready?) Comment positively and specifically on what you're seeing them do, "Your rolling has a nice rhythm to it" or "you made that very very thin." If you feel a need to teach them techniques, make sure children also have time *to freely explore* what clay can do and what it means to them.

Not every child will like all media equally — let your children specialize. Every artist is more comfortable in some media than in others, and we do

---

133. By Cathy Wiseman Topal. Sterling, 1998.

Supply tools and let the artists decide what to do with them

After an initial long period of working with clay without tools, a child may need a butter knife or toothpick or rolling pin. When you perceive this need, you can and should offer this child the tool. We offer tools cautiously, since they can cut off work as well as support it. We must ask ourselves, before we offer a tool: "Will the assistance the tool gives compensate for the interruption of flow?"

Some children go through these stages very quickly, others, more slowly. *Let them.* Pay attention to who *this* child is, and support and observe what's going on. You'll give great help when you're really paying attention.

In Reggio they made a movie of a group of toddlers in diapers — on the floor with a 50 pound block of clay. You could see these tiny children engage with the material, and you could also see the different stages in their work. The children explored the clay for a very long time, perhaps as much as a couple of hours. Impressive!

Providing instruction and materials as needed leaves the children whole and active, creating what they intend to create, rather than passively waiting for the big people to tell them what to do. Working like this is a shift in direction, cultivating agentive children instead of subservient ones. Instead of the adult giving the children work that is of interest to adults, the adult follows the children's interest and direction, and supports it. This shift is a fundamental response to your changing Image of the Child.

A closeup of clay in the classroom

A teacher writes to the Reggio online discussion group about wanting to have children use clay coils (the *snakes or rolls children make in their early explorations of clay*) for making faces. She asks how to get there. There are many steps before children will be ready to do the lesson she's proposing.

The first thing to do, before asking for the clay to be used as lines, is to get to know coils. Give clay to the children with no instructions and no tools. Allow them a long period (maybe weeks) of "messing about." Let this go on until Johnny makes some coils. (Someone always does.) Let's say he makes coils on Monday. The teacher admires them, tells Johnny she'd like him to show the others what he's done tomorrow, and calls them coils (he probably has been calling them snakes).

Don't introduce another medium for several weeks after introducing clay. After the children seem to be really comfortable with clay and have some idea how to make it do what they want, the next step can be to help the children associate a new medium with more familiar ones. When a child has made something he loves in clay, invite him to depict it in paint or drawing as his next step.

For example, if the teacher had, in traditional fashion, suggested Marion move on to slab work, instead of linking her coils to another language, then Marion would have missed out on broadening and deepening her existing understandings. Avoid shifting to the new, at the expense of deepening what we already have. We are not aiming for shallow, but for deep and rich!

There's a thrill in making something you like! Photo: SGC

the range of possibilities fascinating. You can print them a few pictures, but you'll want to set a limit in advance (say, 5) of how many pages you'll print.

For example:  is a very different image from

After discussion and agreement on the general picture the child wants to draw, inquire about the specific problems, "What's the hard part?" Then set up activities which will help the young artist solve those problems. Thinking about these activities is a job for the staff, with lots of input from the children. The discussion of The Crowd Project started with the children's describing their recollections of their experiences in crowds, followed by their first drawings, *drawings that didn't satisfy them. They* knew so much more than they were able to *draw.* Helped by adults, children pinpointed their issues, and the adults set up activities to help them learn. They worked on separate skills until all the things they wanted and needed to do were things they could do.

Much of drawing in Reggio is not solely emotional expression, but *drawing to learn.* The adults are acutely aware that the children may have many different sorts of intentions in drawing, and they work collaboratively and thoughtfully to help each child do what he or she intends. Ursula Kolbe's wonderful book about children and drawing, *It's not a bird yet,*[136] deals brilliantly and at length with this kind of problem.

The teacher must create conditions in which the child draws daily and draws to express or explain her theories. *If I don't keep asking children to draw — to show me what they have in mind —* with the expectation that the drawing will communicate sooner or later, one way or another, *then some children won't ever learn to draw.* This process is *exactly* like talking to a toddler who is learning to speak. Daily drawing helps a child become comfortable with this essential language!

Should we encourage representation? And if we should, then when?

It depends on the child's intention. If he wants to express his experience, then emotional content or ideas or fantasy need not be constrained by realism. If he has a specific image in mind then the closer to actual depiction he comes,

136. Ursula Kolbe, *It's not a bird yet: The drama of drawing,* Peppinot Press, 2005. Also her *Rapunzel's Supermarket: All About Young Children and their Art; Drawing and Painting with Under-Threes; Clay and Children: More than Making Pots; Thinking Eyes: Young Children's Visual Art Experience.*

The Italians tell us to use such observations — something that doesn't seem to make sense — as research provocations, so I began to document. One day some children were making invitations to a party while others were making confetti to go in the invitations. Another day the bits were numbered and used as tickets for a concert the children were planning. On a chilly day they added water to the paper to make soup again. The following week the children created wonderful earrings using tape and the paper bits. One child has begun writing my name and the names of her friends on the bits, galloping into literacy. Now my colleague told me, "When I see your observations and documentation I can see that the children were *not* wasting paper, and I understand why you allow this play." ❧

Responding to the need to conserve paper, staff and parents can talk with children about bringing home only the work they especially want to keep. Parents and staff can discuss Leslie's point that what goes home has a story behind it. Teachers can photocopy children's work when something's wanted both at home and at school. If you give them black and white photocopies most children are willing to add color to a copy. *Keep the original at school.* It will go home eventually, but you will want to display originals (or smaller photos of them) on your documentation panels. A child may need some help to see that leaving some good stuff at school to be hung on the wall or put in his portfolio shows how he's growing and learning. And everyone can pay attention to recycling what isn't needed.

Parents, too, can show respect for their children's work. How you hand children's work to parents at dismissal time matters. If you take 30 seconds to talk about how the child engaged with this drawing (or other artwork) and you provide protection against rain or snow, the work is less likely to be damaged on the way home and the parent's understanding of its value can expand. You might want to get plastic envelopes (large ones) for carrying things between home and school.

More about revisiting

On the Reggio online discussion group, educator Laurie Kocher wrote about listening to what she has recorded in her classroom: ". . . actually hearing the voices again (maybe this is just how my brain works) takes me back to an almost physical presence of the moment — I can see/hear/smell/intuit the experience anew."

Leslie writes:
This is exactly how the children feel when they revisit their experience through documentation! When we fail to revisit important moments with children

Timothy, when we asked him, said "My house got a broken wall, the wall was broken!"

We noted that Alice and Timothy both needed to learn to score and slip clay pieces in order to join them together. After Timothy had learned to score and slip we had find out if Timothy's wall was broken because he wanted to represent a broken wall, or because he didn't know how to fix the wall he had broken.

We showed the children the video a third time, individually, and they had still more to say, two weeks after they'd finished their clay work! With his work and the video in front of him Timothy re-lived the moment and thought out loud about the process. "Here's where the wall is broken. I tried to put it back, but I couldn't, so I left it broken. This part along the wall is broken too!" This use of video is absolutely appropriate for the children, and breaks our general rule of "no screens in programs for young children — no TV, no cartoons, no commercial material — but they can learn from seeing video-tape and photos of their own experience".

Alice said, "This hat fell, and the skirt's wrong," She was having a problem making the brim of the hat rigid so it would look right on the clay girl's head. There was also a problem with the girl's skirt. Alice's sad voice, as she mourned the broken pieces, told us more about why she had suddenly abandoned her work.

Sherman named the parts of his complex piece: "This is a slide, here's the park, this is the Safeway™, here's my house and Kitty's house. I want to put in a boat."

New and different directions emerged because the children made several visits to the documentation of their work, and because we adults gave time and energy to the revisiting process. We heard clues that led us to formulate that the children were wondering, "What is a city?" and "What is a neighborhood?"

What did the children know about their neighborhood and city? Each anchored his or her thoughts in a unique, personal way, and some added an element of fantasy — they moved their friends next door and had their teachers living nearby. The children disagreed among themselves about what was in the city or their neighborhood. Some of the children incorporated ideas from their travels abroad.

Daphne reserves the Getting Ready Legos. Photo: Marie Catrett

Daphne: Reserve for everyone. Even for Elias! He isn't here but (he's still a part of our hearts let-it-be-known).

Once everybody arrives today, we step back into Playing Puppet Show but, unlike the elaborate negotiations that fueled such interesting readiness-making, today the play stalls out right away over intense disagreement and big feelings about who gets to be Baby Rapunzel and who gets to be Grownup Rapunzel. And no, unlike playing Family which often has two mamas, it is decreed that only one grownup Rapunzel can be part of the show. Meanwhile, different thoughts about whether a gray mouse puppet can be in the show undermine the play almost simultaneously. Not working!

I rub some backs and bring everybody to the snack table. Let's refuel and think more about this. I remember I shot seven minutes of video of yesterday's Getting Ready for the Show play and wonder if watching yesterday's play might help us with today? Kids eat, are then very interested to watch the video. Like I saw a week or so ago, the kids are repeatedly surprised by what they see and hear about themselves and will turn to each other to clarify the play on the screen.

Willa: (as she hears herself in the video, surprised) Did I really say 'it's gonna explode?'

Wyatt and Daphne: Yeah!

We watch the entire seven-minute clip.

CHAPTER 49
What makes art authentic?

Authentic art expresses something — intellectual or emotional — that comes from inside the child. It is important that children learn to take their inner images and make them visible or tell them in ways that feel right and good. Much of art instruction in schools in the past has been focused on representing things accurately. Teaching that way can deny the child's intention or vision, sending imagination underground.

Staying out of the decision about what to paint or draw still leaves room for negotiation. If children are making gifts for the forthcoming holiday, instead of the old way: "Children, today we're going to make valentines" a teacher might say, "Some people like to make things for folks they love at this time of year, because of a holiday called Valentine's Day. There are some materials on this table that you might want to use, or if you have other ideas go ahead with them. Whatever you do, I'll be glad to help." If a child completely ignores the idea of valentines, pursuing his own artwork, I'd mention that Mom might very much like something for Valentine's Day, and ask if he would like to give that artwork to her, or ask, "would you like me to write down your words for Mom?"[138]

The art is authentic if the author is the child. The teacher has a responsibility to make sure a variety of art materials become familiar and comfortable languages for children to use. This means regularly inviting the reluctant child who always chooses block building to further acquaint him- or herself with media. "You haven't painted for a long time, and I want you to get to know

---

138. This works only if we know he lives with his Mom. We should be extremely aware of what grownups each child has at home, and perhaps we should say, "please take this to your grownups" rather than "please take this to your parents". The absence of a parent is almost always a source of great pain for children.

The third, marker.

Whatever materials I offered Marcel, he always made a version of this image. I'm fascinated that the image persists and that, years later, even after early childhood, he was still making it.

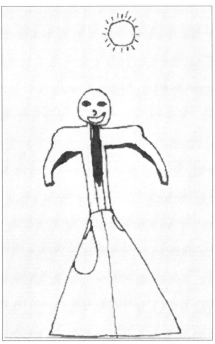

The fourth picture, in marker, made at my request when Marcel was 11.

I've seen other children who kept on drawing the one image for a period of weeks or months: rainbows, or the standard house with the sun and lollipop flowers outside, or superheroes of many sorts. In Marcel's case he's working with an original image (he says it's a friend who he doesn't get to see any more) which has perseverated for more than six years and counting. I believe that Marcel is having a long conversation with himself, of which we can see part of the pictorial record.

His outer life enters his drawings. The ballpoint picture was made when he was in kindergarten, first learning to write. He sometimes attended church with his other grandmother, which may account for the Christ-like posture and the neck-ornament with the cross. I feel the watercolor picture has some elements of superheroes and super-villains in it.

Marcel is skillful at using media: he learns the possibilities of each new one and quickly develops good control. His immediate understanding of media became clear to me as I painted with him the day he made the watercolor image. I tried to produce intense colors like his (we were working with the same tray of paints) and I couldn't!

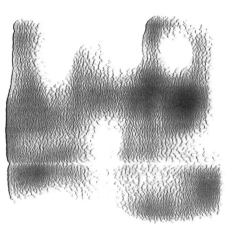

Art is authentic if gender bias isn't playing a role in the child's willingness or unwillingness to engage, if the author isn't fighting an inner belief that painting or wrestling is the province of only one gender. Teachers have a responsibility to free activities from their gender bias. A strategy I've used with boys is: "Can you paint me a really strong painting?" (Likewise, when children are wrestling (surrounded by safety rules and on a padded mat) and some girls demur, I'd ask them "How is wrestling like dancing? What moves are the same?")

In a community where these biases are still common I'd be particularly careful never to call a boy's picture "pretty" — unless he does so first. We can use the masterpieces we find on the web and the stories of their artists (most of those we know about are men, mainly because men have written most of history) to further free our boys to do art without losing what they perceive to be their masculinity.

A colleague on the Reggio Emilia online discussion group wrote that the children in his group participated in an art gallery show of paintings "by artists and children". I wondered what the curators had been thinking — weren't the children artists, too?!

Art is authentic, then, if it is the artists' honest attempt to convey his or her spirit or idea to others, or as the artist's exploration of materials and what they can do. Art, made by anyone at any age, deserves serious attention from the community.

- papers of all sorts, including envelopes
- photocopies or computer printouts of small pictures of the children and adults in the group (to use as addresses)
- glue sticks
- clips
- rulers
- scissors to cut out pictures (and other stuff)
- a set of mailboxes (dividers inside a cardboard carton? something fancier?) with names on them.

Children can leave messages, pictures or other small treasures for each other in the mailboxes, and hopefully some indication of who sent what to whom — or they can confront the problem that they received something and don't know who sent it. You can problematize[139] this!

As the teacher you have a special responsibility — you must reply to all the messages you get, in whatever form — so you need to know who sent them. If you bring the children's attention to your problems with unsigned material, they will develop the habit of signing their work.

All of this activity will help children understand the pleasure of written response and encourage the children to use the writing center more. You can send messages to all the children (don't make them identical) perhaps aiming to send a short message every week to each child.

The Writing Center will underline for the children why we value literacy: we want to know what's what and get messages from folks we like, and writing is another way to do those things!

What do they do with stories in Reggio Emilia?

One of the many remarkable books coming out of the Reggio experience is *The Grammar of Fantasy* by Gianni Rodari, translated into English by Jack Zipes.[140] Rodari, an eminent radical journalist and children's book author, was invited to Reggio Emilia in 1974 to give a series of lectures on how to support children making their own fantasy stories. The fundamental lesson of these lectures is that *stories are made up of other stories*. Once children understand and absorb this idea (and for most children it's obvious) they make up their own, excellent stories. In the service of this goal, Rodari devised many simple techniques for opening children's imaginations — using absurd

---

139. All of *Shoe and Meter*, for example, is the result of having the carpenter provoke the children to supply measurements so he can make them an exact copy of the table they have.
140. Published 1996 by Teachers and Writers Collaborative, NY. English translation by Jack Zipes. The original book was published in 1974.

Once I visited a Bruderhof religious community. They are the people who make the wonderful Community Playthings furniture for early childhood classrooms and while there I went to see their school. Bruderhof children watch no television, but they are told many, many stories, and their library is very rich in picture books and story videos. This is a pacifist community, and war play and war toys are forbidden. While I found their lessons indoors to be quite traditional and formal, with all the children facing front and reciting in unison, these children also had a vast nature area in which they are very, very much at home and freely explore. I invited the four-year-old children to join me in telling stories, and seven chose to come. I started the *Red Meets Gold* exercise and each time I paused the children chimed in.

SGC: "And as she walked through the forest with her little basket of goodies for Grandma, Little Red Riding Hood saw, coming toward her, another girl — with a big head of yellow hair. The girl stuck out her hand and said, 'Hi! I'm Goldilocks.'" "What happened then?"

Child 1: Then Goldilocks said, "What's in your basket?"

Child 2: Red Riding Hood said: "I have goodies for my Grandmother."

Child 1: Then Goldilocks said, "I'm *hungry*."

Child 2: And Little Red Riding Hood said, "This food is for my Grandmother. She's sick."

Child 1: And Goldilocks said, "But I'm *really* hungry."

Child 3: (said in a rush) "And so they sat down and ate all the goodies."

There was a shamed silence in the room after this transgression was spoken. I let the silence go on, and waited for the children's solution.

Child 4: "But there were berries in the woods."

Child 5: "And you can eat nasturtiums, and they grow in the woods."

REMEMBER:

Our deepest fear is not that we are inadequate. Our deepest fear is that we are powerful beyond measure. It is our light, not our darkness, that most frightens us. We ask ourselves, who am I to be brilliant, gorgeous, talented and fabulous?

Actually, who are you *not* to be? You are a child of god. Your playing small doesn't serve the world. There's nothing enlightened about shrinking so that other people won't feel insecure around you. We were born to make manifest the glory of god that is within us.

It's not just in some of us; it's in everyone. And as we let our own light shine, we unconsciously give other people permission to do the same. As we are liberated from our own fear, our presence automatically liberates others.

—Rev. Marianne Williamson, from her book: *A Return To Love: Reflections on the Principles of A Course in Miracles (1992)*, quoted by Nelson Mandela in his 1994 Inaugural Speech

It's the artists of the world, the feelers and thinkers, who will ultimately save us, who can articulate, educate, defy, insist, sing and shout the big dreams.

—Composer and conductor Leonard Bernstein

I never teach my pupils, I only attempt to provide the conditions in which they can learn.

— Scientist Albert Einstein

The ultimate aim of education is to take each one out of his isolated class, and into the one humanity.

— Social activist, educational critic, poet and philosopher Paul Goodman

Dahlberg, G.& Moss, P. & Pence, A. (1999/2007). *Beyond Quality in Early Childhood Education and Care:* Postmodern Perspectives. London, UK: Falmer Press.

Davis, B.& Sumara, D. & Luce-Kapler, R. (2008). Engaging Minds: Changing Teaching in Complex Times. New York: Routledge.

Dewey, J. (1933/1960). *How we think.* Lexington, MA: Heath.

Dewey, J. (1944/1961). *Democracy and Education.* NY: Macmillan.

DeVries, R. et.al. (2002). *Developing constructivist early childhood curriculum: Practical principles and activities.* NY: Teachers College Press.

Donovan, M. & Sutter, C. (2004). "*Encouraging doubt and dialogue:* Documentation as a tool for critique." Language Arts, vol. 81 no. 5.

Edwards, C. & Gandini, L. & Forman, G., eds. (1998). *The hundred languages of children:* The Reggio Emilia approach—Advanced reflections (2nd ed). Greenwich, CT: Ablex Publishing.

Edwards, C. P. & Rinaldi, C. (2008). *The Diary of Laura:* Perspectives on the Reggio Emilia Diary. St. Paul, MN: Redleaf Press.

Eisner, E.W. (1994). The Educational Imagination: On the design and evaluation of school programs, 3rd ed. NY: MacMillan.

Felstiner, S. et al. (2006). "The Disposition to Document" in Fleet, A. et al. *Insights: Behind early childhood pedagogical documentation.* Australia: Pademelon Press.

Fife, B. (1998). "Questions for Collaboration: Lessons from Reggio Emilia." Canadian Children, vol. 33 no. 1.

Fillippini, T. & Vecchi, V. (1996). Catalog of the 100 Languages of Children Exhibit, Reggio Emilia, Italy:, Reggio Children.

Fleet, A. & Patterson, C. & Robertson, J., eds. (2006). *Insights: Behind Early Childhood Pedagogical Documentation.* NSW, Australia: Pademelon Press.

Forman, G. (1989). "Helping children ask good questions." Neugebauer B. ed. The wonder of it: Exploring how the world works. Redmond, WA: Exchange Press.

Freire, P. (2004). *Pedagogy of Hope,* London, UK: Continuum Press.

Fu, V. & Hill, L. & Stremmel, A. 2001. *Teaching and Learning:* Collaborative Exploration of the Reggio Emilia Approach. Upper Saddle River, NJ: Prentice Hall.

Gandini, L. (1993). "Fundamentals of the Reggio Emilia approach to early childhood education." *Young Children,* (Journal of the National Association for the Education of Young Children) vol. 49 no. 1.

Gandini, L. & Cadwell, L. & Hill, L. & Schwall, C. (2005). *In the spirit of the studio:* Learning from the atelier of Reggio Emilia. NY: Teachers College Press.

Gandini, L. & Edwards, C.P., eds. (2001). *Bambini: The Italian Approach to Infant/Toddler Care.* NY: Teachers College Press.

Gandini, L. & Etheredge, S. & Hill. L., eds. (2008). *Insights and Inspirations:* Stories of Teachers and Children from North America. Worcester, MA: Davis Publications, Inc.

Ginsburg, H.P. & Asmussen, K.A. (1988). "Hot Mathematics" in Saxe, G. & Gearhart, M. eds. Children's Mathematics. New Directions for Child Development, SF: Jossey-Bass.

Goldhaber, J. & Smith, V. R. (2002). "Application of the Reggio Emilia approach to early childhood science curriculum." *Early Childhood Education Journal,* vol. 30, no 3.

Goldhaber, D.E. & Goldhaber, J. (1996). "Theory Guided Early Childhood Teacher Education," presented at the *1996 Piaget/Vygotsky Centenary Conference,* Brighton, UK.

Malaguzzi, L. (1994). "Your Image of the Child: Where Teaching Begins." *Child Care Information Exchange,* March, 2004.

Mitchell, N. (2010). *University Students' Perceptions of Pedagogical Documentation: A Qualitative Research Study.* M.A. Thesis, East Carolina University.

Milliken, J. (2003). *Reflections:* Reggio Emilia Principles Within Australian Contexts. NSW, Australia: Pademelon Press.

Moss, P. (2010). "What is your image of the child" *UNESCO policy brief on Early Childhood #47.*

New, R.S. (1989). *"Projects and Provocations:* Preschool Curriculum Ideas from Reggio Emilia, Italy." ERIC document. *http://www.eric.ed.gov/PDFS/ED318565.pdf*

New, R.S. (1993). "Reggio Emilia: Some lessons for U.S. educators." ERIC Digest. Champaign, IL: ERIC document. *http://www.eric.ed.gov/PDFS/ED354988.pdf*

New, R.S. (2000). "Reggio Emilia: Catalyst for change and conversation." ERIC document. *http://www.ericdigests.org/2001-3/reggio.htm*

Noddings, N. (2005). "Caring in Education" *The Encyclopedia of Informal Education.* *http://www.infed.org/biblio/noddings_caring_in_education.htm*

Oken-Wright, P. (2001). "Documentation: Both mirror and light." *Innovations in Early Education: The International Reggio Exchange,* Vol.8 No.4.

Oken-Wright, P. (1998). "Transition to Writing: Drawing as a Scaffold for Emergent Writers." *Young Children,* (Journal of the National Association for the Education of Young Children) March, 1998.

Paley, V. G. & Coles, R. (1991). *The Boy Who Would Be a Helicopter,* Harvard University Press.

Paley, Vivian Gussin

Wally's stories. (1981) Boston, MA: Harvard University Press.

Boys and girls: Superheroes in the doll corner. (1984). University of Chicago Press.

Mollie is three: Growing up in school. (1988). University of Chicago Press.

Bad guys don't have birthdays: Fantasy play at four (1988). Chicago, IL: University of Chicago Press

White teacher. (1989). Boston, MA: Harvard University Press.

The boy who would be a helicopter. (1991). Boston, MA: Harvard University Press.

You can't say you can't play (1993).

Kwanzaa and me: A teacher's story (1995). Boston, MA: Harvard University Press.

The girl with the brown crayon. (1997). Boston, MA: Harvard University Press.

The kindness of children. (1999). Boston, MA: Harvard University Press.

In Mrs. Tulley's room: A child-care portrait. (2001)

A child's work: The importance of fantasy play. (2004). University of Chicago Press

The boy on the beach: Building community through play. (2010). Chicago, IL: University of Chicago Press.

"Plowden Report" *Children and their primary schools: A report of the central advisory council for education. London: Her Majesty's Stationery Office, 1967.* *http://www.dg.dial.pipex.com/documents/plowden.shtml*

Pacini-Ketchabaw, V. & Prochmer, L. (2013). Re-Situating Canadian Early Childhood Education. NY: Peter Lang Publishing.

Pile, N.F. (1973). Art Experiences for Young Children. NY: Macmillan.

APPENDIX

Appendix A:
Building or buying a light table

There should be about 24-36 linear inches of table per child, so think about that when building or buying a table. A parent made our wonderful table (30" x 72") for about 350 dollars, back in 1992. It's just a box on sturdy legs at standing height — the height I had seen in Italy. Inside the box are energy efficient light bulbs, outside the box there's a switch. There are holes in the bottom to vent the heat of the bulbs, and the top is made of fairly heavy translucent Plexiglas™. It's not a difficult job for any competent carpenter. The light should be evenly distributed, with no "hot spots" or shadows. As many as six children could work around it comfortably.

Appendix B:
Using the kaleidoscope

Another tool we see in Reggio Emilia is the Kaleidoscope. It allows one to see oneself multiplied and divided by mirrors, providing a novel and evocative experience, one that helps children think about why and how they're seeing so many images of themselves and others.

This kind of provocation expands the number of perspectives a child can consider. When we had a kaleidoscope in our classroom, we could see the children puzzling about it, crawling inside to hang out with their (also multiplied) friends in snug groups of two and three.

In Diana School, one was located in the piazza (a large central, internal room where people gather for meetings). Sensibly, one kaleidoscope was shared by the whole school (75 children in three classes) since the apparatus takes up a fair amount of floor space and isn't always in use.

Shared equipment needs a plan for optimal, trouble-free use. Will adults determine how many children may enter at a time, or will the children decide? Will you decide how many can play inside the kaleidoscope at once, or will you problematize sharing this space?[1] Why? How will turns be taken? Do you use waiting lists? Must shoes be removed to protect the mirrors? One community has determined that four barefoot children may be in the kaleidoscope at one time, and they've provided a place where exactly four pairs of shoes can be stored next to a waitlist. Adults may decide to organize the area at first, but later the question of how many can be problematized for the children to consider. Adjustments and further refinements will come after you've observed the children, and listened to what they have to say about the many reflections they see — the flowers they, and their friends, become!

---

1. See problematization section, *pages 128-130*

Appendix E:

Children's books about death and grief

It's a good idea to introduce the subject of death *before* a family or community must deal with a loss, so children have some idea what it's about. When we encounter a dead bug or bird, or worm or anything, it's a good time to do some reading, since learning by doing is out of the question.

It's good to read *Lifetimes* by Brian Mellonie when a dead bug is found, or when the fish dies. It helps to have read it *before* grandma is dying. A book can provide a framework to think about things that are not directly accessible. Children will experience death, and we can prepare them for that encounter by reading and discussing such a book with them.

Following death, there's grief. Children grieve in fits and starts, and between times, they play. The younger they are, the longer their immature, sporadic grieving will take. Adults should be aware that a very young child who seems to have recovered from grief is likely to resume grieving sooner or later. A beautiful book about grief is *My Grandson Lew*, by Charlotte Zolotow, in which a child and his mother remember grandfather long after he's gone. A book, particularly suitable for four- to six-year old children, is *Jim's Dog Muffins*, in which the first grade children and their teacher are concerned about Jim, who is grieving for his dog, who was run over by a car. The book depicts both helpful and unhelpful ways of befriending a grieving child, and the wise teacher sums it all up, "Maybe Jim just needs time to be sad."